RAPID REACTION FORCES

RAPID
REACTION
FORCES

Fast, hard-hitting and élite

Patrick Allen

Airlife
England

Copyright © 2002 Patrick Allen

First published in the UK in 2002
by Airlife Publishing Ltd

British Library Cataloguing-in-Publication Data
  A catalogue record for this book
  is available from the British Library

ISBN 1 84037 271 0

Typeset by Rowland Phototypesetting Ltd,
Bury St Edmunds, Suffolk
Design by Celtic Publishing Services, Wrexham
Printed in Hong Kong

Airlife Publishing Ltd

101 Longden Road, Shrewsbury, SY3 9EB, England
E-mail: airlife@airlifebooks.com
Website: www.airlifebooks.com

CONTENTS

INTRODUCTION

In today's unpredictable strategic environment, the major Western powers are turning towards the use of hard-hitting, flexible and easily deployable forces that must be able to undertake a full range of missions at extremely short notice. Although tensions between the super-powers have diminished, there is now a greater requirement for the international community to intervene in regional conflicts anywhere in the world, helping to contain and even prevent hostilities. This new policy of international policing has increased the need for highly specialised mobile forces that can be deployed anywhere and operate either independently or as part of a larger joint or combined force.

Both the United States and the United Kingdom have invested heavily in recent years to create rapid reaction forces. By adapting their airborne, air assault and amphibious forces, they have established specialist spearhead units capable of rapid reaction. These include the UK's new 16 Air Assault Brigade and Amphibious Task Group, and the US Ranger, Airborne and Air Assault Divisions combined with the US Marine Corps' Marine Expeditionary Units (MEU).

European forces have also been turning towards rapid reaction capability within Nato's multi-national division (central) – the European focus for air manoeuvre doctrine and training – and by the creation of a new European Rapid Reaction Force (ERRF). This book takes a look at some of these new rapid reaction forces, along with their equipment and aircraft.

CHAPTER 1
16 Air Assault Brigade

As a result of its strategic defence review and the initial success of the joint rapid reaction force concept in 1996, the UK set out to create a more capable, better-supported rapid reaction force with the kind of strategic and tactical back-up transport that would make it easily deployable. This led to the creation of the UK's 16 Air Assault Brigade and the Royal Navy's Amphibious Task Group. These, together with a pool of other units, form the nucleus of a rapid reaction force which can be called upon at short notice to mount medium-scale operations of all kinds. These fall under either national auspices, such as Operation *Palliser* in Sierra Leone, or under Nato, the United Nations or the European Union as part of the new European Rapid Reaction Force (ERRF). The spearhead of the UK's new rapid reaction capability is 16 Air Assault Brigade.

The brigade was formed on 1 September 1999 from the UK's 24 Airmobile Brigade and 5 Airborne Brigade to create the country's first air manoeuvre unit. This unique operation within the British Army involves more than 8000 personnel from all three services. It is highly capable and rapidly deployable, combining all the elements of airmobile and airborne warfare doctrine. The brigade offers

An aircrew man marshals a quad-bike ridden by a paratrooper from 16 Air Assault Brigade into the back of a Chinook at the start of a 16 Air Assault Brigade exercise. The quad-bike and paratrooper were later deployed from the Chinook in darkness to lay a series of infra-red runway lights to guide-in the lead C130 Hercules during a night tactical air-land operation.

RAF Chinooks lift forward an air-portable forward-area refuelling system to refuel attack helicopters at the start of an assault by 16 Air Assault Brigade. Troops from the US Army's 101st Airborne Division (Air Assault) can be seen in the background waiting to be flown forward.

wide-ranging combat power to deal with all sorts of situations, from humanitarian and peace-keeping operations, to full conventional warfare, working independently or as part of a coalition force. It is one of the four formations assigned to Nato's multi-national division (central), and marks an important step in the development of air manoeuvre capabilities within both Nato and the ERRF.

A mixed fleet of attack and battlefield helicopters, together with the RAF's tactical air transport fleet, provides the brigade's tactical air manoeuvre and firepower capability. These assets, together with the use of airborne and specially-trained air assault troops, enable the brigade to undertake a full range of helicopter-borne and parachute missions. The cornerstone is the helicopter force, which includes the new Agusta-Westland WAH-64D Apache Longbow attack helicopter, designated as the Apache AH1. This provides the brigade with formidable, flexible, hard-hitting and highly mobile firepower. The Apache operates alongside other land or air units to secure or open points of entry for them.

16 Air Assault Brigade is a key element of the UK's new joint helicopter command (JHC) formed on 1 October 1999, also as a result of the strategic defence review. The command brings together 12 000 personnel from all three services, and more than 350 battlefield helicopters. It coordinates and plans all training and resources across the three services to ensure maximum support for the units under its jurisdiction. While continuing to maintain the ethos of the individual services, the focus of the JHC is on joint force capabilities, thereby enhancing

the operational effectiveness of the helicopters and air assault forces.

The headquarters of 16 Air Assault Brigade are at Colchester in Essex. The main element of the brigade is its air assault troops, two parachute battalions and an air assault infantry battalion. One of the two parachute battalions retains a parachute capability, while the other two provide air-land and 'heliborne' infantry support. Combat support and combat services support units, which provide reach, mobility and sustainability, add to the brigade's strength. The arrival of the Apache AH1 has given the brigade's operational capabilities a considerable boost, providing the mobility, flexibility and combat power necessary for long-range offensives including joint air-land missions.

Helicopters and tactical transport aircraft give the brigade its airlift and strike capability, allowing it to combine the best of both airborne and airmobile elements. Transport aircraft provided by the RAF are the Boeing C-17 Globemaster, Hercules C130Js and C1s and C3s which are used for parachuting or air-land assault through tactical air-land operations (TALO) and rapid air-land operations (RALO), both of which can also involve heliborne assaults.

Using this air capability, the brigade is ideally positioned to undertake air manoeuvre operations, making the most of both rotary and fixed-wing assets. As part of these, the Apache will undertake joint air attack missions (JAAT), operating within a larger force, under a strategy known as combined air operations (COMAO). The brigade has been expanding its COMAO planning to include night missions, and taking part in these are airborne command and control units such as the E-3D Sentry, tanker refuellers, and unmanned aerial vehicles (UAVs). Their roles include reconnaissance, air defence, suppression of enemy air defence, and close air support. Many of these aircraft types will regularly support the brigade on long-range night missions to seize and secure airfields before other forces follow. 16 Air Assault Brigade conducts almost all its operations at night and regularly trains for this type of mission.

The brigade provides the UK with a unique military capability; it is equipped for a wide range of missions as

An Army Aviation Lynx Light-Battlefield Helicopter (LBH) lands at the tactical headquarters of 16 Air Assault Brigade during Eagle's Strike. *The brigade headquarters, like everything else in the new brigade is airportable and capable of moving at a moment's notice.*

the spearhead of the country's joint rapid reaction force, and will certainly be first into any area of conflict.

Units within 16 Air Assault Brigade

Headquarters personnel include 35-strong RAF detachment
216 Signal Squadron (Air Assault)
Pathfinder Platoon
Household Cavalry troops
7 Parachute Regiment, Royal Horse Artillery
21 (Gibraltar) Battery, Royal Artillery
23 Engineer Regiment, Royal Engineers
Explosive Ordnance Disposal Troop, 33 Engineer Regiment
The Parachute Regiment, 1st, 2nd and 3rd Battalions
1st Battalion, The Royal Irish Regiment

13 Air Assault Support Regiment, Royal Logistics Corps
7 Air Assault Battalion, Royal Electrical and Mechanical Engineers
132 Aviation Support Unit, Royal Logistics Corps
16 Close Support Medical Regiment, Royal Army Medical Corps
156 Provost Company, Royal Military Police

Aviation Units

Joint Helicopter Command
3 Regiment, Army Air Corps (Lynx and Apache)
4 Regiment, Army Air Corps (Lynx and Apache)
9 Regiment, Army Air Corps (Lynx and Apache)
RAF Support Helicopter Force

The Eagle is the emblem of the UK's new 16 Air Assault brigade and is worn by all members of the Brigade.

A paratrooper from 2nd Battalion Parachute Regiment wearing his 16 Air Assault Brigade's Eagle patch waits for his Chinook to move forward during Eagle's Strike which took place in Scotland in July 2000.

Satellite communications are essential in modern air manoeuvre operations and are used by the UK's 16 Air Assault Brigade.

A 27 Squadron RAF Chinook moving in to pick up a 7.6 ton Scimitar armoured reconnaissance vehicle (tracked) from the Household Cavalry Regiment who are part of 16 Air Assault Brigade.

ABOVE: *A 105 mm gun team from 7 Parachute Regiment, Royal Horse Artillery about to fire live rounds across the Canadian Prairies having just been flown into position by RAF Chinook helicopters.*

OPPOSITE: *An RAF 18 Squadron Chinook lifting out a 105 mm gun, a Pinzgauer 4x4 vehicle plus ammunition belonging to 7 Parachute Regiment, Royal Horse Artillery.*

BELOW: *Lead aviation and reconnaissance units from 16 Air Assault Brigade deployed to the Canadian prairies east of Calgary in September 2000 during exercise* Iron Hawk. *An 18 Squadron Chinook HC2 is seen flying-in bridging equipment for 51 Air Assault Squadron, Royal Engineers, watched over by an armed WM1K Land Rover.*

ABOVE AND BELOW: *One of the UK's new RAF C17 Globemaster IIIs seen at Seeb airport during the UK's Rapid Reaction Force exercise* Saif Sareea 2 *which took place in Oman in late 2001.*

CHAPTER 2
16 Air Assault Brigade – Advance Operations
(TALO Pathfinders)

With today's emphasis on fast-reaction operations in potential trouble spots anywhere in the world, 16 Air Assault Brigade needs to be able to get its forces into position perhaps several hundred miles from a forward base, which may itself be thousands of miles from Britain. The brigade's priority is to establish and secure a position from which to conduct subsequent operations. These may be anything from peace-keeping to full-scale conventional warfare.

The entry point is usually an airfield, military or civilian, or any place that would allow a large number of Hercules transports to land and take off. These aircraft can airlift the entire brigade and supply and resupply it with food, fuel and ammunition. Helicopters can fly in under their own power, or be airlifted by Boeing Globemasters.

The brigade regularly practises seizing a landing ground under cover of darkness. This is the first task in any combat zone, and involves a combined air operation leading to a tactical air-land operation; in other words, heliborne assault troops clear the airfield before the arrival of Hercules aircraft with supplies. Only then will the main bulk of the brigade arrive, using rapid air-land operation tactics to quickly build up its strength.

A fleet of RAF C130 Hercules arrive back at the main staging area having successfully completed a night tactical air-land and rapid air-land operation to deploy the lead elements of 16 Air Assault Brigade into an airhead. Once refuelled the C130s will continue to build-up the combat power of the brigade as they conduct their operations.

An RAF C130 Hercules from No 47 Squadron, flown by a USAF exchange pilot, seen at low level over the Oman desert during the UK's Rapid Reaction Force exercise Saif Sareea 2.

Gurkha troops still form an important part of UK frontline units including 16 Air Assault Brigade. This sniper is waiting to board his C130 Hercules for a night TALO to secure an airfield along with Pathfinder troops.

Airfield assault

Several weeks before an operation advance forces will be sent into the theatre of operations to be the main force's eyes and ears. These include troops from the Pathfinder platoon who can be parachuted in or flown by RAF Chinook helicopters. These specialist troops are part of the brigade's intelligence, surveillance, target acquisition and reconnaissance (ISTAR) capability. The technological elements of ISTAR include satellite imagery, airborne stand-off radar (ASTOR), unmanned aerial vehicles (UAV) fast reconnaissance jets, and the Apache's fire control radar (FCR) and radar frequency interferometer (RFI) together with secure digital data-links to other units.

TALO assault

A tactical air-land operation is used to put a small but powerful assault force into a target area by using an existing runway, grass strip or other flat ground capable of taking Hercules C130 aircraft. Operating entirely at night, two RAF C130 C1s equipped with night vision cockpit lighting and full defensive aids suite (DAS) lead the first assault, along with heliborne troops carried in by RAF Chinooks which can land where they choose in the surrounding area.

Each TALO aircraft carries a 7.6 ton Scimitar armoured fighting vehicle from the Household Cavalry equipped with a 30 mm cannon, plus thirty air assault troops and a Land Rover armed with a machine-gun. The C130 flies a very low approach for maximum surprise, and, on landing at the target strip, comes to a quick stop so troops and equipment can be rapidly unloaded, ideally within two minutes. The aircraft then departs. The troops' role is then to secure the runway and surrounding area. They may also be backed up by a parachute drop. Some troops will deal with enemy forces, while others will lay out landing lights for the other Hercules which will be in-bound once they get radio clearance. Within minutes the brigade can have a large number of troops on the ground, still under cover of darkness, backed up by Apache AH1s. Meanwhile, close air support will be provided by RAF Harrier GR7s, Tornado GR4s and Jaguars.

The initial TALO assault is the culmination of a well-orchestrated combined air operation, which can involve up to seventy aircraft whose sole purpose is to gain an entry point to the target area.

A Household Cavalry Regiment Scimitar armoured vehicle is backed into the hold of the TALO C130 Hercules and together with a WM1K armed Land Rover plus thirty troops is the first to hit the ground to prepare the runway for follow-on C130s. The entire mission is conducted at night.

ABOVE: *The first C130 Hercules to land are the TALO aircraft flown on night vision goggles (NVGs), each loaded with a WMIK Land Rover and Scimitar-armoured vehicle plus thirty troops to seize the runway and prepare for the arrival of the rapid air-land C130s. The TALO is supported by attack helicopters and combined Chinook heli-assault.*

BELOW: *A pair of paratroopers riding quad-bikes wait to board their Chinook at the start of a 16 Air Assault Brigade mission to seize an airfield. Their role was to ride out of the Chinook and lay infra-red runway lights for the C130 TALO aircraft.*

Pathfinder troops fast-rope from an RAF Chinook rehearsing for a night assault. Using three ropes, over forty troops can deploy from a Chinook in under one minute.

ABOVE: *An RAF E-3 Sentry AEW1 lifts off to support a 16 Air Assault Brigade air manoeuvre exercise. The Sentry has several key members of the brigade aboard and is vital in coordinating all the air elements involved in a multi-aircraft mission, which includes fast-jets, transport aircraft and helicopters.*

BELOW: *An RAF Tornado F3 forms one part of a combined air operation involving RAF fast-jets, close air support, suppression of enemy air defences and command and control, all supporting 16 Air Assault Brigade to accomplish its various missions.*

ABOVE: *A Pathfinder WMIK Land Rover is driven aboard an RAF Chinook before being flown forward for a reconnaissance mission. Pathfinders are deployed many days prior to a mission and are the eyes and ears of the brigade. They provide vital strategic and tactical reconnaissance material for the brigade.*

BELOW: *A Phoenix UAV is prepared for flight. Unmanned vehicles are becoming an important method of gathering intelligence information as well as target acquisition.*

The Royal Artillery operates the Phoenix battlefield surveillance and target acquisition unmanned vehicle. This is the first unmanned vehicle operated by the British Forces.

OPPOSITE: *Unmanned vehicles are now being used by advanced forces to help them gather information. Their role in the future, especially within 16 Air Assault Brigade, will become increasingly important. Future roles will include unmanned vehicles operating as a team with the Apache AH1. Armed unmanned vehicles are now entering service with the US Army.*

ABOVE: *Known as Magic the RAF E-3 Sentry AEW1 is a major player in UK combined air operations. The Sentry coordinates all the air assets within the brigade.*

BELOW: *16 Air Assault Brigade relies on combined air operations to undertake many of its missions. This includes RAF Tornado GR4s which provide SEAD and close air support for the slower transport and helicopters.*

ABOVE: *Pilots prepare their Harrier GR7s, Jaguars and Tornados for a major combined air operation during exercise NITEX 2000 at RAF Leuchars, Scotland, the first major night COMAO to support 16 Air Assault Brigade.*

BELOW: *RAF Jaguar pilots start their aircraft for a COMAO mission to support 16 Air Assault Brigade. They will work as part of a team involving over 40 aircraft, plus C130 Hercules and helicopters in a timed to within a minute operation to take an airfield in west Scotland all under the control of an RAF E-3 Sentry.*

CHAPTER 3
16 Air Assault Brigade – C130 Hercules Para Assaults

Once cleared for landing, the Hercules C3 and C1s from RAF Lyneham arrive at one-minute intervals. To get maximum combat power on the ground in the shortest possible time, up to twelve C130s unload as quickly as possible and immediately return to the forward base to reload with more supplies. During the initial stages of an operation the brigade can be entirely resupplied by RAF Hercules. The principle is that all the brigade's equipment can be ferried on the C130s. This includes aviation fuel for the helicopter fleet, with a Hercules taking on a forward air refuel equipment (FARE) role as a fuel station, or depositing its load into large fuel bladders provided by the RAF's tactical supply wing (TSW).

There will be about a hundred air movements a day as the brigade builds up its logistical strength. Once the initial operation has been completed, C130s will continue to fly in, providing the necessary logistical support. Their next task will be to fly the brigade out when its operation is complete, either back to the forward base or to another target zone for a further assault.

Paratroopers from 16 Air Assault Brigade line-up with their kit waiting to board their C130 Hercules for a daylight parachute assault.

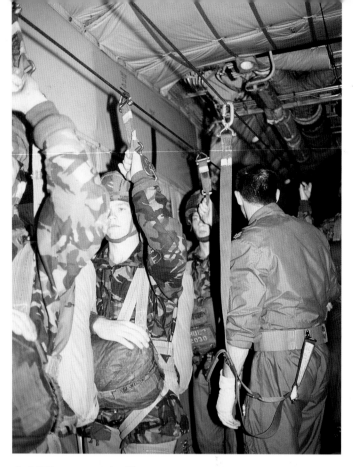

An RAF jumpmaster checking paratroopers as they wait for the green light having already connected up their static lines.

A C130 Hercules is travelling at around 115 knots during a parachute drop. This image shows a paratrooper exiting the port-side door. During a jump both doors are used simultaneously.

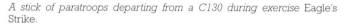

A stick of paratroops departing from a C130 during exercise Eagle's Strike.

British paratroopers seen using the Irvin low-level parachute and jumping from 250 ft. The paratrooper has already extended his Bergen/kit from a line for the landing.

ABOVE: *Paratroopers seen trying to collapse their canopies as they are dragged along the ground in windy conditions.*

RIGHT: *Cargo parachutes carrying sixteen one-ton containers about to land on the drop-zone.*

As well as delivering paratroopers, RAF C130 Hercules can also deliver ammunition and stores by parachute.

Crews watch a one-ton container to confirm that the parachute has opened safely.

LEFT: A paratrooper being given a gentle nudge by the jumpmaster, as he is about to exit the port-hand para-door of a C130.

CHAPTER 4
16 Air Assault Brigade – Para Assault

16 Air Assault Brigade has absorbed, adapted and expanded both the airmobile and airborne doctrines to suit its various operational needs. Two of its three parachute battalions retain a parachute capability, which they can integrate with the air-land and heliborne infantry assault forces. The brigade can also bring in vehicles and other heavy equipment by parachute. Each C130 can drop two medium stressed platforms (MSP) per trip, with a weight of 18 000 lb each, or a single heavy stressed platform (HSP) with a weight of 35 000 lb. While resupplying the ground forces' stores, the crews can transport sixteen one-ton containers in the Hercules C1 or twenty-four in the stretched C3. They can also use the ultra-low level air drop system (ULLADS), by which a 14 000 lb platform is dropped from a C130 flying at 30 ft above the ground.

The main force is dropped into the target zone by the low-level parachute (LLP) method at night, from an altitude of 250 ft. The C130J/C5 or C130 C1 can carry sixty-two fully-equipped paratroopers, while the stretched C130J/C4 or C130/C3 at 15 ft longer, can carry eighty-eight fully-equipped paratroopers. They can also deploy a 'wedge' container carrying 3000 lb of ammunition and or rations from the rear ramp.

Large-scale airborne operations are no longer considered effective, but movements on this scale as part of a larger operation can bring a tactical advantage. This is especially the case with the securing of a landing zone, when a parachute assault can split the enemy and distract him from the main attacking force. Night parachute assaults, when the enemy has limited vision, can also be useful in getting forces on to the ground quickly.

A crew of a C130 Hercules preparing for landing at the airhead during a rapid air-land mission.

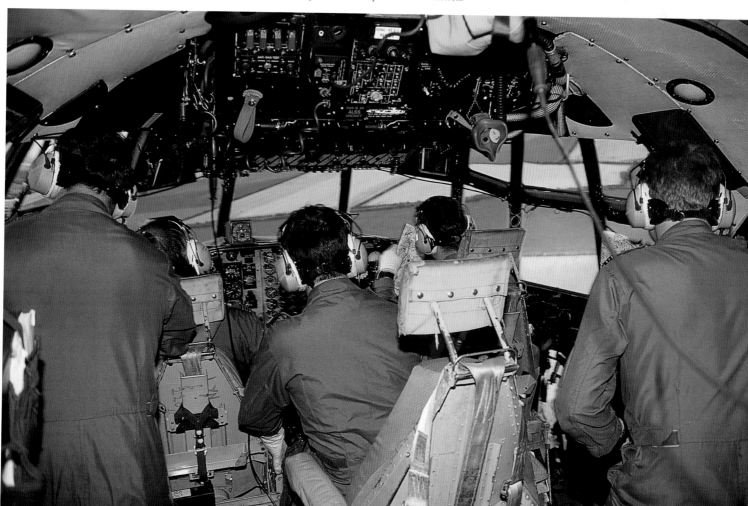

ABOVE: *RAF C130 Hercules about to touchdown at an airhead. The C130 Hercules is the workhorse of 16 Air Assault Brigade, undertaking a wide range of missions. All the brigade's assets are capable of being flown in a C130.*

BELOW: *Building up combat power on the ground as quickly as possible is the role of the C130 Hercules during rapid air-land. A fleet of over twenty C130s are used to support 16 Air Assault Brigade.*

ABOVE: *A paratrooper talks on a satellite radio while a constant supply of C130s arrive during the initial phase of the rapid air-land phase. As long as the brigade holds the airhead C130 Hercules will conduct regular resupply runs bringing in ammunition and equipment.*

BELOW: *As well as C130 Hercules, the Chinook is also used to help move equipment from the airhead to the forward units.*

ABOVE: *Troops run off their C130s during the initial phase of the rapid air-land with the first wave usually comprising around fifteen C130s all arriving within one-minute intervals. As soon as they are offloaded they depart immediately for the next run.*

OPPOSITE TOP: *C130 Hercules wait at the airhead to load-up paratroopers for a follow-on mission whilst a 27 Squadron Chinook helps to move equipment and troops away from the airfield.*

OPPOSITE BELOW: *Having established an airhead the whole operation is done in reverse once the brigade has completed its mission or prepares to launch another air assault onto another airhead. Vehicles are seen lined-up waiting to be loaded for another mission.*

CHAPTER 5

16 Air Assault Brigade – Army Aviation

The cornerstone of the 16 Air Assault Brigade is its helicopter force including the new WAH-64D Apache Longbow made by Agusta-Westland. The helicopter is based on Boeing's AH-64D Apache Longbow, and provides the brigade with formidable fire-power.

The UK's Apache differs from the Boeing version in that it has: two Rolls-Royce Turbomeca RTM322 twin-shaft engines; a back-up-control system; a performance monitoring system; a blade anti-icing system; a BAE Systems defensive aids suite; Saturn and Bowman secure speech radios; and Canadian CRV7 rockets.

The UK ordered sixty-seven Apaches, with forty-eight of them to be operated by three army aviation regiments within 16 Air Assault Brigade. Of the other nineteen Apaches, eight will be operated by No 651 Squadron, the Apache operational training and conversion unit at Middle Wallop; two will be retained for development and system trials, based at Middle Wallop and Boscombe Down; while the remaining nine aircraft are to be stored to provide replacements.

The Lynx AH7, and the light battlefield helicopter Lynx AH9, will also serve in the three army aviation regiments.

Army Lynx AH7s and LBH9s seen in a massed formation. Both types will continue in service for several more years working alongside the Apache AH1.

By the end of 2001, the Army was to have decided on a replacement for the Lynx. This would either be an upgraded model of the present Lynx AH7/9, or a different helicopter, with models such as the Bell 412 being considered.

The forty-eight Apaches will be divided among six squadrons, with eight Apaches each. Each army aviation regiment will also have a light utility helicopter squadron (using the Lynx AH7/9 or its replacement). All three regiments should be fully operational by mid-2005, forming an aviation battlegroup.

The regiments are:

3 Regiment, Wattisham, Suffolk
662 Squadron: eight WAH-64D Apache Longbow helicopters
663 Squadron: eight Apaches
653 Squadron: Lynx AH7s and AH9s

4 Regiment, also based at Wattisham
654 Squadron: eight Apaches
669 Squadron: eight Apaches
659 Squadron: Lynx AH7s and AH9s

9 Regiment, based at Dishforth, Yorkshire
656 Squadron: eight Apaches
664 Squadron: eight Apaches

9 Regiment is also set to provide one squadron of Apaches to join the UK's Amphibious Task Group on HMS *Ocean*. This is the country's new Landing Platform Helicopter vessel (LPH), where the Apaches will be working alongside RAF Chinooks and Royal Navy Commando Sea Kings and Merlins as part of the Tailored Air Group.

16 Air Assault Brigade intends to deploy its Apaches for three specific roles – attack helicopter raids, armed reconnaissance, and air manoeuvre. They will use a mixture of weapons, and will provide the brigade with its principal weapons system.

The Lynx AH7 will retire from the anti-tank role but will continue in service, equipped with door-gun and sighting system, undertaking the light battlefield and utility role in support of the Apache AH1.

ABOVE: *An army aviation squadron command post being flown forward by Lynx LBH9s. Army aviation is taking an increasingly important role in conducting aviation-led raids and deep strike missions within 16 Air Assault Brigade.*

BELOW: *Lynx AH7s from 3 Regiment Army Air Corps seen forward deployed at a 16 Air Assault Brigade airhead during the Eagle's Flight exercise.*

A Lynx LBH9 pilot checks his aircraft at the start of the day during a 16 Air Assault Brigade exercise. Army and RAF helicopter crews now work and operate under a single Joint Headquarters.

Attack Helicopter Raids

'Deep operations' are missions in which Apaches are given the task of taking out specific far-off targets, probably behind enemy lines.

The Apache has a range of more than 155 miles, and this can be extended by using forward arming and refuel points (FARPs). RAF Chinooks will refuel the Apaches using their 800-gallon Robertson extended range tanks (ERTs) and forward area refuelling equipment. One Chinook can carrying three ERTs providing 2400 gallons of fuel. Another Chinook may carry missiles and ammunition. This allows the Apaches to hold a position close to the target before launching an attack, with the availability on-hand for rearming and refuelling either during the mission or on the return to base. Apache raids can be covert and quick, or can be mounted in conjunction with other air power such as close support fast jets, or perhaps even with artillery.

Armed Reconnaissance

The Apache is ideally suited to the armed reconnaissance role, using its fire control radar (FCR) together with the radar frequency interferometer (RFI), an integrated surveillance system for detecting enemy radar.

The FRC prioritises the top sixteen targets in ground targeting mode, and separates the 128 most important targets into tracked or wheeled vehicles, or air defence systems. All this information, which is fully digitised through the battle management system, can be sent back to ground commanders, passed on to other Apaches, or to airborne information gatherers such as the AWAC, giving information from the front line or from behind enemy lines that is bang up to date. The Apache's technology will provide a huge leap forward in the intelligence, surveillance, target acquisition and reconnaissance capabilities of 16 Air Assault Brigade.

Air Manoeuvre

In the air manoeuvre role, Apaches will operate in an aviation battlegroup, often in large numbers and as part of a combined force of other air and land units such as

All army aviation pilots are trained to operate on night vision goggles (NVGs) and Lynx pilots leave their training squadron with a basic CAT: a qualification to fly down to 200 ft above ground level (AGL). Modern military helicopter pilots can expect to use NVGs throughout their flying career.

armoured vehicles, multi-launch rocket systems (MLRS) and artillery. The aim would be to achieve domination within a specific area of operation.

In the air manoeuvre role, the Apache will be the primary battlefield weapons unit, using its ISTAR systems and its speed, range, manoeuverability and fire-power to dominate the battlefield. To sustain its position there, 16 Air Assault Brigade can carefully orchestrate its Apaches to provide twenty-four-hour cover. Helicopters at the front can be switched with others held on quick reaction alert status.

Air-Land Arming and Refuelling Points

Air and forward arming and refuelling points (ALARPs)

allow the brigade to mount air- and infantry-led raids deep behind enemy lines. The ability to quickly establish an operating base far into enemy territory, one where the brigade's helicopters and Harriers can rearm and refuel, is vital.

Refuelling with the C130 ALARP

Using standard RAF C130 C1s or C130Js, a forward refuelling point can be set up within minutes of the aircraft touching down, bringing around 26 tons of aviation fuel. The fuel is pumped from the C130's tanks via an outlet located on the outside of the fuselage, and the aircraft's loadmasters connect the four 50 ft hoses and direct the work. This sort of work is almost always carried out at night, with crews wearing night vision goggles.

A Hercules refueller can be used to supply Chinooks, as they fly ahead in turn to rearm and refuel other helicopters and Harrier GR7s.

Because fuel is carried in the Hercules' own tanks, space inside is left clear for a security team. This usually comprises two armed Land Rovers and up to forty troops, whose job it will be to protect a site of operation as well as to look after the teams who load missiles and shells on to Apaches and Harriers.

Almost any suitable landing site can be used for an ALARP. The site would usually be checked out by an advance force such as the Pathfinders, who will provide lighting for the approach and make sure the area is clear of enemy troops. Beaches are a favourite site for ALARPs.

Depending on the mission and the amount of fuel used, the C130 can get airborne and top-up its tanks in air-to-air refuelling, before returning to the landing site. During larger strikes, a C130 ALARP will provide support for Chinooks operating in the forward arming and refuelling point (FARP) role, in which they accompany the Apaches close to their area of operations. Allowing the Apaches to refuel, and rearm close to their strike area, means a faster turnaround during a mission. Taking turns to refuel and rearm means the Apache teams can continually engage the enemy.

Chinook FARPS

RAF special forces Chinooks have been using their FARP capability since the Gulf War. This is now being used by the brigade in almost all its air assault missions. With the arrival of the Apache AH1, the Chinook will become increasingly important in support of attack helicopter raids.

Unlike the C130, the Chinook needs extended range tanks so it can carry additional fuel for other helicopters. These are usually a pair of Robertson 800-gallon ERTs, plus forward area refuelling equipment, which includes hoses and a pump providing 120 gallons per minute from two pressure points.

With two ERTs installed, the Chinook can carry a FARP security team or about fifteen personnel, with the Apaches providing an escort and checking out the FARP site before the Chinooks arrive.

As with the C130 ALARP, a Chinook FARP takes minutes to establish and close down.

The Apache provides the UK with a formidable weapons system, and 16 Air Assault Brigade and other army aviation units are continuing to expand and exploit the helicopter's capabilities. The Apache AH1 is expected to provide the British Army with thirty years' service.

ABOVE: *The Apache AH1 attack helicopter entered service with the British Army in 2001. The helicopter will be the cornerstone of future air assault operations.*

BELOW: *The UK Apache AH1 is armed with a 30 mm chain gun that can fire 1200 armour-piercing or high explosive rounds.*

ABOVE: *The UK Apache AH1 can carry a mix of CRV7 rockets and two types of Hellfire missiles, either semi-active laser-guided or Radio Frequency millimetric providing a true fire-and-forget capability.*

BELOW: *Army Lynx refuel from a C130 Hercules air-land arming and refuelling point (ALARP) during a 16 Air Assault Brigade deep strike mission. The new brigade is exploiting the ability of both Chinooks and C130 Hercules to refuel and rearm the Apache AH1 during these types of missions.*

ABOVE: *A Lynx AH7 seen being refuelled from a Chinook during a 16 Air Assault Brigade aviation raid. It takes only a few minutes for the Chinook to land and deploy up to two refuel hoses at any suitable pre-arranged landing site.*

BELOW: *A Chinook crewman ready to turn off the fuel pump during a FARP mission. The Chinook can carry up to three 800 gallon extended range fuel tanks plus pumps and hoses to refuel helicopters, vehicles or Harrier aircraft.*

A Lynx being refuelled at a Chinook FARP. The Chinook can deploy two hoses and refuel two aircraft simultaneously. The whole procedure from landing to take-off can take only a few minutes and is a real force multiplier.

CHAPTER 6
16 Air Assault Brigade – RAF Support Helicopter Force

As part of the UK's joint helicopter command, the RAF support helicopter force provides 16 Air Assault Brigade with essential back-up, moving troops and equipment around the battlefield. As part of the joint force concept, RAF support helicopters operate as an integral part of the system, and undertake a full range of missions within the aviation battlegroup. These range from long-range covert reaction of advance forces and Pathfinders, to moving assault troops into position, transferring guns during artillery raids, and supporting Apaches during deep-penetration raids. The support helicopter fleet is the workhorse of the brigade, and is involved in every aspect of its operations. The RAF operates a fleet of Boeing Chinook HC2s and HC3s, the Agusta-Westland Puma HC1, and the new Agusta-Westland Merlin HC3.

RAF Chinook Wing
7 Squadron, RAF Odiham: Chinook HC3s
18 Squadron, RAF Odiham: Chinook HC2s/HC2As
27 Squadron, RAF Odiham: Chinook HC2s
33 Squadron, RAF Benson: Puma HC1s
28 Squadron, RAF Benson: Merlin HC3s

The RAF Puma HC1 will continue to operate alongside the newer Merlin HC3 for several more years.

ABOVE: *A Puma HC1 deploys a reconnaissance unit from 16 Air Assault Brigade during an exercise. The Puma is fast and agile and capable of carrying around ten fully equipped troops.*

LEFT: *An RAF 18 Squadron Chinook seen ripple-firing a salvo of infra-red flares. The RAF Chinook fleet is well protected with the latest in aircraft survivability equipment.*

ABOVE: *A Chinook aircrew man operating one of two M134 Miniguns during a mission. The Miniguns can fire over 6000 rounds per minute.*

RIGHT: *A head-on shot of a 27 Squadron Chinook HC2 showing the two missile approach warners on the forward pylon.*

ABOVE: *A joint helicopter support unit (JHSU) team connect a one-ton Pinzgauer and trailer to be flown out of the airhead on a 16 Air Assault Brigade exercise.*

BELOW: *Night-time NVG cockpit view of an RAF Chinook crew about to depart on a mission showing their NiteOP goggles and lead counter-weights fitted to their helmets.*

ABOVE: *Paratroopers board their Chinook to be flown forward from the airhead during a 16 Air Assault Brigade exercise on the island of Islay in Scotland. A Chinook can be seen in the background refuelling another Chinook (FARP) on the edge of the Atlantic Ocean.*

BELOW: *'If you can't take a joke you shouldn't have joined': RAF Chinook crews seen trying to plan a night mission in a water-logged tent during a 16 Air Assault Brigade exercise.*

ABOVE: *A pair of RAF Chinook HC2s in close formation. The Chinook has exceeded all operational expectations. Its role in future air manoeuvre missions supporting the Apache AH1 will be vital.*

BELOW: *British and German paratroopers seen waiting for their Chinook to fly forward from the airhead. 16 Air Assault Brigade works regularly with other airborne/air assault units from Europe and the USA.*

ABOVE TOP: *An RAF Merlin HC3 from No 28 Squadron formally entered operational service in July 2001 and will work alongside the Chinook and Puma supporting 16 Air Assault Brigade.*

BELOW: *Having been forced by politicians to take the Merlin for political and not operational reasons the RAF is beginning to exploit the Merlin's capabilities.*

Originally purchased for the Chinook special forces flight during the Gulf War the Robertson extended range tanks (ERTs) and forward area refuelling equipment (FARE) is now used extensively by 16 Air Assault Brigade to help extend operational capabilities. This role will be used to enhance the range and capability of the new Apache AH1.

CHAPTER 7
16 Air Assault Brigade – Exercise *Eagle's Strike*

In the summer of 2000, 16 Air Assault Brigade under-took its first large-scale air manoeuvre exercise in Scotland. There was an exercise in Canada as well where an aviation battlegroup operated on the prairies, testing new concepts and preparing for the arrival of the Apache AH1. Exercise *Eagle's Strike* in Scotland included a large-scale combined air operation and airfield seizure.

During exercise *Iron Hawk* in Canada, parts of the brigade including Chinooks and army aviation battle-group personnel conducted night operations within a live-fire training area, under the context of a joint rapid reaction force (JRRF) deployment.

Eagle's Strike began with a combined air operation to seize an airfield on the west coast of Scotland, kicking off with the words, 'All stations this is Magic, code word Krypton'.

An RAF Boeing E-3D Sentry AEW passed the code-word to the air elements of the assault force, including Army Lynx and RAF Chinook helicopters, C130 Hercules transport aircraft and Jaguar, Harrier and Tornado fast jets. The codeword told them that air reconnaissance, as well as the prying eyes of the special forces and Pathfinders, indicated that they should push on towards the target.

The mission was to seize the airfield using a combined parachute, air-land and heliborne assault. Timing would be critical to the mission, which had already involved fast jets and helicopters carrying out reconnaissance,

A flight of Lynx from 3 Regiment Army Air Corps returning to the airhead from an air assault mission, about to refuel from a C130 Hercules.

suppressing enemy air defences, and providing escort and close air support. Hercules transports, meanwhile, delivered paratroopers from the 2nd Battalion, the Parachute Regiment, before the start of a Hercules rapid air-land operation. As the wheels of the first TALO C130s touched the runway, four RAF Chinook HC2s from No 18 Squadron were simultaneously deployed at four pre-selected landing sites along the airfield perimeter. They carried a company of troops of the US Army's 101st Airborne Division (Air Assault), based at Fort Campbell, Kentucky. Their mission was to pinpoint the enemy on the airfield, allowing attack helicopters, fast jets and para-troopers to attack them. The airfield would be secured, and the brigade would build up its strength on site.

From the starting point of the mission, an airfield in Gloucestershire, timings were to the second. The four Chinooks were given a window of only two minutes in which to deploy their troops on the perimeter, and they had to coincide with the TALO Hercules. Their landing sites were also within the parachute drop zone, and any delay would jeopardise this part of the mission.

The operation also involved attack helicopters creating minimum-risk, five mile-wide, special army aviation flight routes (SAAFR) for the low-level C130s, Army Lynx and RAF Chinooks which were cleared to fly as low as 50 ft off the ground.

ABOVE: *RAF 18 Squadron Chinook lifting fuel hoses for a forward refuel point during exercise* Eagle's Strike.

BELOW: *RAF Chinook and army aviation crews are briefed at a forward position on the Canadian Prairies for a night mission during exercise* Iron Hawk *in September 2000.*

RIGHT: *A 27 Squadron Chinook HC2 moving a Pinzgauer and trailer to a forward location during exercise* Eagle's Flight, *the first major 16 Air Assault Brigade exercise.*

BELOW: *An RAF 33 Squadron Puma HC1 deploying a Pathfinder team during exercise* Eagle's Strike *in Galloway, Scotland.*

A 16 Air Assault Brigade airborne command element (ACE) aboard an RAF E-3D worked with the brigade commander in his Lynx Helicopter, and oversaw the entire COMAO. Before the main assault, Chinooks were given the job of establishing an FARP fifty miles from the target area for the Lynx and Gazelle helicopters.

The entire mission was carefully planned and orchestrated with strict segregation by time, geography, and height; helicopters were not allowed above 200 ft, to keep them away from fast jets and C130s operating down to 250 ft. Pre-selected codewords, which formed a mission execution checklist, informed each element about any change to the original plan and when they were cleared to push forward. All this took place under the watchful eye of the ACE aboard the E-3D. With the Paras, C130s, Chinooks, Lynx and fast jets all arriving at the specified objectives at the allocated times, the assault plan was a major test of the skills of the brigade's planners.

Much of the brigade's new air-assault doctrine is based around the COMAO principle, using the relevant air assets of the RAF and Army to help achieve its aims. Exercise *Eagle's Strike* was used to develop and expand

this multi-element capability, as two large-scale COMAOs set about taking an airfield as an entry point before the rest of the mission ensued. Day and night, aviation-led battle group raids and strikes were conducted, combining air assault, air strike and artillery bombardments to first find, pindown and then destroy the enemy, with Lynx AH7 helicopters acting in the role of the Apache. Missions included airborne reconnaissance, escorting and protecting troop-carrying Chinooks, and deep strikes by joint artillery and attack helicopters (JAAT) forces.

The exercise involved more than 1200 troops. Among them were A Company, 3rd Battalion, 502nd Infantry Regiment, 101st Airborne Division (Air Assault); four RAF Chinooks from No 18 Squadron at RAF Odiham; a Puma from No 33 Squadron, RAF Benson; and eight RAF C130

The high velocity missile or HMV is deadly to helicopters and low flying aircraft. Each missile has three darts, each capable of destroying fast-moving targets. This shows a live firing during exercise Iron Hawk *in Canada.*

Hercules as well as three USAF C130 Hercules. No 4 Regiment, Army Air Corps, from Wattisham, operating TOW-armed Lynx AH7s, Lynx AH9s and Gazelles, also took part.

The joint Army/RAF helicopter fleet operated from individual forward operating bases (FOBs) with crews living in field conditions during the exercise. An 18 Squadron Chinook pilot joined 4 Regiment as a liaison officer to help plan the aviation-led battle group raids, which included a 4 Regiment-led night operation with heliborne, attack helicopter and artillery elements to destroy an enemy force in the Galloway hills.

The main objectives of the exercise were to practise being part of an airborne aviation task force in an expeditionary environment within a Nato context. It also involved deploying a temporary tactical brigade headquarters, whose role was to combine an aviation and airborne task force with elements of the RAF in planning and executing battle tactics including air manoeuvre operations in a low to medium intensity environment. Practice centred on massed parachute jumps, TALO and aviation-led battle group operations, coordination of army aviation and RAF

support helicopters and the execution of combined support helicopter, air assault and aviation operations by day and night.

The brigade made maximum use of new technology such as satellite imagery to obtain photographs of target areas and enemy positions. Chinook and Lynx crews also used computer-generated 3D imagery of the terrain; this helped with planning their initial point (IP) and concealed approach and departure (CAD) routes. Designated SAAFR or a nearby aircraft control point (ACP) helped route them to their IP.

Prior to each mission, intelligence teams furnished crews with the latest information on known enemy air defences and their arcs of fire. Several sorties were made using terrain masking to get underneath known ZSU23/4 (Anti-aircraft Gun) dangers, with Chinooks flying low and slow to achieve their objectives. Army and RAF pilots took

A Household Cavalry Regiment Samson armoured reconnaissance vehicle (tracked) being flown by an RAF Chinook. This is the view through the centre hatch.

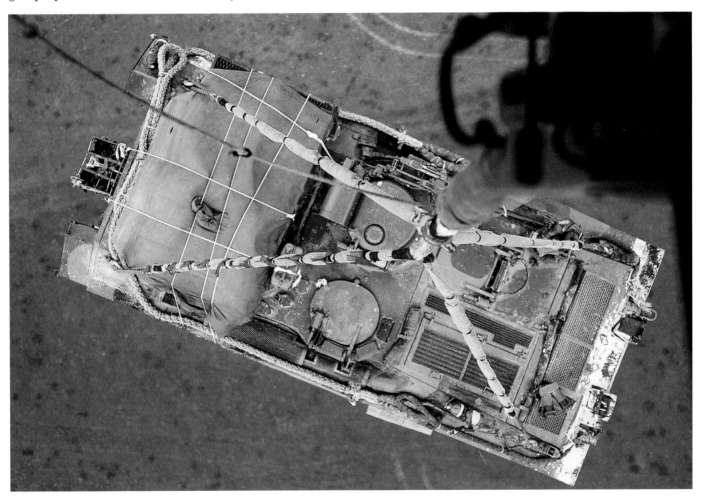

the opportunity to compare their IPs using both 3D technology and good old-fashioned map-reading, with Army and RAF pilots both choosing the same routes.

For major COMAOs, helicopter and C130 crews could also make use of the Hercules' joint mission planning computer, which had the details and positions of all the aircraft involved. All helicopter crews used the system to plan their routes for the second COMAO.

Once the route, waypoints, ground speed and ETA at the target had been entered, the system provided exact route timings, and a colour map would be printed for each crew. Whenever possible, face-to-face briefings would take place with the commanders of each aircraft element, to help coordinate planning and ensure there would be no conflict over routes. This was particularly important for Army and RAF helicopter crews and those of the C130 Hercules, who would be operating in the same airspace at the same time.

The exercise helped prove that the brigade was combat-ready for its joint rapid reaction force role; it had been able to carry out the swift planning and execution of several operations over a week-long period of both day and night. Four major missions and several minor ones had been set up and completed. A major headache for all

those who take part in such exercises is keeping aircraft a safe distance from each other, while still achieving the operations' goals, but detailed COMAOs planning enabled all helicopter types, fast jets, transport aircraft, and artillery to be used to full effect with minimal risk of harm to the troops and aircrew.

At one stage, the brigade launched a major aviation-led night attack to destroy an enemy force in the Galloway hills. The mission required advance reconnaissance by the Pathfinders, and the deployment of forward air controllers by Lynx helicopters to help locate enemy air defences and other targets, and to establish a look-out.

During late afternoon, Chinooks flew 105 mm light artillery to a forward position, while Lynx crews undertook armed reconnaissance patrols. At 22:00 hrs, four Chinooks with part of 2 Para, escorted by Lynx AH7s,

A Chinook lifts out of Carlisle airport with a triple load at the start of the largest 16 Air Assault Brigade exercise, Eagle's Strike, *which took place in July 2000.*

ferried the paratroopers to pre-selected landing sites which had been secured by Lynx crews.

The mission included a joint artillery and attack helicopter strike, while other Lynx provided a protective screen for incoming Chinooks. Meanwhile, Harrier and Tornado aircraft provided close air support, while being ready to engage any enemy air defence or ground units. The mission also required the establishment of a FARP by Chinooks. The Mission Commander in his Lynx oversaw the entire operation. There was also a company of Gurkha paratroopers waiting in reserve at West Freugh.

The exercise ended with the brigade being brought out of the arena to Carlisle. A second COMAO and assault also took place on Watton airfield in East Anglia, four hundred miles to the south-east. Like the first mission, this was timed to the second under the watchful eye of an E-3D Sentry, and involved a combined TALO and heliborne assault with an accompanying parachute jump, while fast jets provided combat air patrols, escort duties, close air support and enemy air defence suppression.

It all showed that 16 Air Assault Brigade was working hard to develop expertise in new concepts such as the COMAO, especially the night-time version, as well as developing strategies for the Apache. Within their first year, sections of the brigade and their Chinook support helicopters had seen service in Kosovo and Sierra Leone and had conducted several night COMAO assaults.

Paratroopers wait aboard their Chinook for the 'H' Hour. In wartime the seats would be removed to allow even more troops to be flown. If the flight time is not too long troops stand with over eighty paratroopers packed into a single Chinook.

ABOVE: *A Chinook refuels from another Chinook during exercise* Corsican Lanyard, *which involved deploying paratroopers around the Isles of the Scottish west coast.*

BELOW: *Royal Irish Regiment troops from 16 Air Assault Brigade secure the perimeter around a Chinook during exercise* Eagle's Flight *in 2000.*

CHAPTER 8
UK Rapid Deployment to Sierra Leone

Operation *Palliser*, the British operation to evacuate expatriates when civil war erupted in Sierra Leone in May 2000, was a text-book example of the rapid reaction concept. It involved a large force from the 16 Air Assault Brigade and the Amphibious Task Group, led by HMS *Ocean*.

The RAF's air transport and Chinook support helicopter fleets were instrumental in the fast deployment during *Palliser*. A massive airlift was undertaken, first to deploy paratroopers from the spearhead 1 Para and then to support the troops once in the field. RAF C130 Hercules from RAF Lyneham and RAF TriStars from 216 Squadron at Brize Norton were the backbone.

A forward mounting base had to be set up at Dakar in Senegal followed by a RALO using C130 Hercules and paratroopers to Lungi international airport in Sierra Leone. The original plan had been to mount a joint air-land and parachute assault to secure Lungi, but this was rejected on political grounds.

A fully armed No 7 Squadron Chinook HC2 seen over typical Sierra Leone jungle.

OPPOSITE: *A No 7 Squadron Chinook lands on a river sandbank. The Revolutionary United Front (RUF) rebels exploited river systems to enable them to move more easily around the country.*

BELOW: *During the operation Lungi international airport near Freetown was the main airhead for both British military and the United Nations.*

The arrival of four RAF Chinooks at Lungi within 36 hours of first being told to deploy from their UK base 3000 miles away is now military folklore. The arrival of the Chinooks in time to meet up with the lead elements of the rescue force was vital to the eventual success of Operation *Palliser*. They first took entitled civilians out of Freetown, the capital, then secured Lungi airport and the surrounding areas. More missions were to come.

Scramble the Chinooks

At around midday on Friday 5 May 2000, the Chinook wing at RAF Odiham, in Hampshire was told to consider the possibility of being sent to Sierra Leone. By 15:00 they were asked to provide an officer who would join an advance reconnaissance team being sent to the region. At 20:00 the same day, RAF Odiham received orders to send two Chinooks 3000 miles to Sierra Leone to support 1 Para in the evacuation of civilians from Freetown.

The first two Chinooks from No 7 Squadron left Odiham just hours later, at 07:00 on Saturday 6 May followed by the second pair early the following morning. The speed of the operation meant that aircraft and ground crew had to be recalled from exercise in Scotland, with engineers working non-stop to prepare the aircraft for their mission. The whole of the base, including headquarters staff and all three operational squadrons, 7, 18 and 27, were involved.

The Chinooks were equipped with two 800-gallon Robertson extended-range tanks, and each aircraft had replacement crews from all three squadrons who would help in the transit – the farthest self-deployment in the history of RAF helicopter squadrons. As diplomatic

ABOVE: *A 7 Squadron aircrew man operates his 7.62 mm M134 Miniguns as another Chinook deploys a patrol close to a river. The Chinooks were the main workhorse and took part in both hostage rescue missions.*

BELOW: *The Chinook not only self-deployed to Sierra Leone but became the workhorse for UK operations, flying patrols throughout the region and operating from Royal Navy Task Force ships.*

Royal Marine Commandos return to their 846 Naval Air Squadron Sea King after a jungle patrol.

clearances to fly over countries en route were being obtained, the first two Chinooks were ordered to go to Gibraltar.

By early Sunday the Chinooks, flown by crews from No 7 and 18 Squadrons, left Gibraltar for Faro on the southern tip of Portugal, there to refuel before heading to Tenerife in the Canary Islands. Again they took on fuel and changed crews for the long night flight of more than 815 miles to Dakar on the West African coast. Arriving at 21:00 on the Sunday, the Chinooks were reconfigured from their ferry designation into their fully armed one. They left Dakar for the final three-hour transit down the coast to

Sierra Leone, reaching Lungi airport at first light on Monday 8 May.

The two No 27 Squadron Chinooks left Odiham on Sunday morning, heading directly for Faro then down to the Canary Islands. There they, too, changed crews for the sea crossing to Dakar, and then it was on to Sierra Leone. As well as being the longest self-deployment by RAF Chinooks, it was also one of the fastest, with each aircraft flying more than twenty-three hours within a thirty-six hour period.

During the journey the Chinooks provided mutual search and rescue support for their long sea transit, with pilots wearing night vision goggles. They also varied their altitude to take maximum advantage of favourable winds.

Meanwhile, the ground support teams were arriving by C130 transports to prepare the Chinooks for immediate work.

By early Monday evening the bulk of 1 Para, reinforced by elements of 2 Para – a total of more than 800 men and their equipment – had arrived at Lungi by C130 and 216 Squadron TriStars. Four TriStars had been used to help fly the troops and their equipment on the six-hour journey from the UK to Dakar, where eight RAF C130s and thirteen crews from all five RAF Lyneham squadrons then flew the Paras down to Lungi airport. With the support of various logistical and specialist teams, such as the UK's Mobile Air Movement (MAM), Tactical Medical Wing, RAF Regiment and RAF Police, along with other operation, administration, communication and supply outfits, more than 100 sorties were flown day and night into Freetown during the initial phase, with each round-trip lasting more than four hours.

On the first night, the Chinooks, having spent the afternoon deploying the Paras to secure and consolidate their positions at Lungi airport, started flying them from the airport across the wide river estuary to Freetown to prepare for the evacuation of UK and other entitled civilian personnel.

An evacuation reception centre was established at the Mammy Yoko Hotel situated on the Aberdeen Peninsula just outside the capital. The hotel was also being used by United Nations staff, who had set up a helicopter landing site just a few hundred yards away, with a second site used by the World Food Organisation located close by.

By late Monday evening, the two 7 Squadron Chinooks began the non-combatant evacuation operation (NEO),

Crews man their Miniguns during a jungle patrol. There was a real threat of RAF helicopters being engaged by RUF rebels and they came under fire during both hostage rescues.

A pair of 7 Squadron Chinooks land on a river sandbank to deploy troops. These sandbanks provided useful landing sites in the more dense jungle regions.

flying the civilians from the hotel to Lungi airport and then by C130 to the base at Dakar. The Chinooks and Paras evacuated more than 300 personnel during this first phase.

This being successfully completed, the Paras began to extend their operations, by first finally securing Lungi airport and the peninsula. This allowed UN staff to continue using the airport for operations within Sierra Leone without risk of attack by the Revolutionary United Front (RUF) rebel group. At one stage, the airport faced attack by RUF forces. The timely arrival of the British provided much needed moral support to both the UN and the hard-pressed Sierra Leone Army (SLA) which had been involved in fighting the RUF throughout the region.

UK forces had a limited role; they were not deployed to the region to fight alongside the SLA, but to provide technical and logistical support. They had strict rules of engagement, and could attack only if fired upon by the RUF. Their main role was to protect the airport and Freetown areas, and to bring out civilians. This involved sending troops forward so they could warn about possible RUF attacks.

The Chinooks were constantly busy during the deployment, undertaking day and night missions to resupply patrols and provide the rapid response needed by the quick reaction force. They also provided a casualty evacuation capability, and helped deploy a number of Jordanian troops assigned to the UN when they arrived in the area. With the arrival of the Royal Navy task force and more than 700 Royal Marines on HMS *Ocean*, the Chinooks were then involved in landing the marines and their equipment, including their 105 mm guns.

For their mission in Sierra Leone, the Chinooks were armed with a pair of M134 Miniguns in the forward door and hatch, and an M60 machine-gun mounted on the aft

OPPOSITE: *A 7 Squadron Chinook launches a salvo of anti-missile flares.*

BELOW: *Flares are deployed to counter an infra-red missile system and can be launched manually or automatically when connected to other counter-missile systems such as missile approach or radar warners.*

ramp. They were also equipped with additional armour-plating to provide protection from small arms fire. On their arrival, they conducted a fire-power demonstration with their two Miniguns and M60s close to known RUF positions, letting the rebels know what they might expect should they take on a Chinook with ground fire.

By mid-May the Paras had largely secured the region around Freetown, with the SLA gaining ground even in RUF strongholds. This was helped by the capture of the rebel leader Foday Sankoh by SLA and British troops near Freetown. A Chinook flew him to a secure location, while on the same day Paras from the Pathfinder platoon, engaged RUF forces near Lungi airport. A Chinook was given the task of evacuating a wounded female civilian

who had been caught up in the fighting, back to the casualty reception centre at the airport. By 25 May the four RAF Chinooks had flown more than 350 hours during 200 missions.

The Royal Navy task force that arrived in mid-May comprised the aircraft carrier HMS *Illustrious*, the helicopter carrier HMS *Ocean*, with more than 700 Royal Marines from 42 Commando, plus the frigate HMS *Chatham* and three Royal Fleet Auxiliary ships. It allowed a relief operation to take place, replacing the Paras with Royal Marines. This was completed by Sunday 28 May.

The arrival of HMS *Ocean* provided the operation with an additional five Royal Navy Commando Sea King HC4s and armed Lynx AH7s, as well as Gazelles. With the Royal

A UN chartered Antonov arriving at Lungi with more vital supplies. The RAF Chinook detachment was also based at Lungi.

Navy helicopters, a joint RAF/Navy helicopter force was established at Lungi to deal with daily movements. Once the Royal Marines had successfully established themselves ashore, the two No 27 Squadron Chinooks and their air and ground crews embarked on HMS *Ocean* on the Sunday along with the Quick Reaction Force, becoming part of the ship's Tailored Air Group (TAG), with No 7 Squadron continuing to operate from Lungi airport. No 27 Squadron was already familiar with the ship, having been the first RAF Chinook squadron to embark on the helicopter carrier during exercise *Bright Star 99*.

Operation *Maidenly*
By early June, No 27 Squadron had returned to the UK,

with HMS *Ocean* leaving the region around 15 June. No 7 Squadron personnel and two Chinooks remained at Lungi to assist in training SLA troops and to assist in the rescue of the one remaining UK national, Major Andrew Harrison. Major Harrison was one of eleven UN observers taken hostage by the RUF in early May and then released to the 220 Indian troops forming the UN garrison at Kailahun, which then came under siege from the RUF.

On 15 July No 7 Squadron Chinooks were used to air-lift British soldiers as well as Indian UN troops into Kailahun to rescue the besieged UN forces and Major Harrison. The rescuers came under heavy RUF fire, but no one aboard the helicopters was injured. A few days after the mission, No 7 Squadron returned to RAF Odiham.

Operation *Barras*
From RAF Odiham, three 7 Squadron Chinooks went on self-deployment back to Sierra Leone on Sunday 27

August with crews from No 18 and No 27 Squadrons. They were to participate in the rescue of six British and one Sierra Leonean soldiers taken hostage by the Westside Boys rebels and held at their stronghold 45 miles east of Freetown, called Gberi Bana. This was separated by the Rokel Creek, from Magberi village where heavily armed reinforcements from the Westside Boys were based, within firing range.

This combined Army, Navy and RAF rescue mission involved 150 members from A Company, 1 Para, special forces and two Army Lynx AH7 helicopters from 657 Squadron, along with RAF C130 Hercules transports. The Hercules from No 47 Squadron provided an ALARP for the Lynx and Chinooks based on a tactical landing site at Hastings, as they had done during Operation *Maidenly*.

Operation *Barras* was launched at 05:45 on Sunday 10 September, with a heli-assault by the three No 7 Squadron Chinooks supported by two Lynx AH7s armed with door-mounted 0.50 in FN machine-guns. Their task was to provide close air support and ground fire suppression.

During the assault two 7 Squadron Chinooks with heavily-armed special forces and Paras attacked Gberi Bana while the third Chinook simultaneously deployed Paras at Magberi. All three Chinooks came under heavy ground fire. This was neutralised by the Lynx and Chinooks which fired more than three thousand rounds each.

During the early part of the assault, several team members sustained injuries, and there was one fatality.

As one of the Chinooks lifted away with the hostages from Gberi Bana, the pilot received a radio call to pick up the wounded paratroopers on the other side of the creek at Magberi, and managed to land nearby to pick them up. The casualties were in operating theatres aboard RFA *Sir Percival* within twenty minutes. After fierce fighting, which lasted forty minutes, the assault team cleared the area and were extracted by midday. By Tuesday 12 September they were back in the UK followed soon after by 7 Squadron and its Chinooks.

The success of the British operation, especially during the early stages when the rebels were in a position of strength, was largely due to the rapid deployment of large numbers of paratroopers, and the ability of the Chinook

Having flown in from HMS Ocean *a pair of 846 Naval Air Squadron Commando Sea Kings arrive to deploy a jungle patrol of Royal Marines.*

HMS Ocean, *seen here anchored off Freetown, provided much needed relief for the Paras who had been in the country for several weeks and were replaced by the Royal Marines.*

support helicopters to be in position waiting for the first C130 Hercules to arrive.

It is no exaggeration to say that the Chinook was crucial to the ultimate success of the mission. The fact that four were able to self-deploy more than 3000 miles within 36 hours of being given notice to move, and their ability to run smoothly throughout the mission, is a credit to their engineering ground crews, and to the support that the detachment received from the Chinook wing at Odiham and from the new joint helicopter command. The Chinook was already a legend within the British forces and loved by the soldiers who rely on it; this operation only enhanced the helicopter's reputation.

The RAF air transport fleet flew mission after mission throughout the operation. Part of it involved Operation *Basilica* in late May, under which at least one flight a day was flown from the UK with a C130 always deployed at Lungi at any one time, and the remainder based at Dakar to fly personnel and equipment whenever and wherever they were needed.

With the end of Operation *Barras* in September, a British amphibious task group returned to Sierra Leone in mid-November for Operation *Silkman*. HMS *Ocean* led the operation, carrying a full Tailored Air Group which included two 18 Squadron Chinooks and a Commando group.

The mission was to deter RUF rebels once more with a sudden appearance off the coast. It lasted from 10 to 20 November, and involved amphibious exercises at sea, an amphibious landing, and further exercises on the Aberdeen peninsula, while resupplying UN and British troops well inland and around Port Loko. It also included a demonstration of fire-power at Hastings and Waterloo, and a feint against an enemy island position. The task group was back in the UK by Christmas.

ABOVE: *A UN Mi-17 Hip departing Lungi airport on another mission in support of the UN troops in the region.*

BELOW: *The Sierra Leone Army operated two Mi-24 Hinds flown by mercenary pilots. The Hinds proved highly successful in countering RUF activity against helicopters.*

Having replaced the Paras the Royal Marines took over their WMIK Land Rover seen here operated by Royal Marines armed with a 0.50 in machine-gun and a 7.62mm general-purpose machine-gun (GPMG).

CHAPTER 9
US Rapid Reaction Forces

The United States has the world's largest strategic rapid deployment force, capable of deploying large numbers of troops anywhere in the world at short notice. The bulk of this capability is based around the US Army's Special Operations Command, comprising special operations groups and the 75th Ranger Regiment, along with the 18th Airborne Corps. This Corps, with its headquarters at Fort Bragg, North Carolina, comprises the 82nd Airborne Division and 101st Airborne Division (Air Assault).

The 82nd Airborne Division are airborne specialists with their own helicopter support, and the 101st Airborne Division (Air Assault) are the world's only air assault division combining organic helicopter and ground forces to conduct manoeuvre warfare. All these units rely on United States Air Force (USAF) Air Mobility Command to provide their strategic and tactical airlift capability.

The Marine Corps is also an integral part of the rapid deployment concept, providing marine expeditionary units (MEUs). These are based around their Large Helicopter Dock (LHD), Landing Platform Helicopter

Rangers undertaking Special Purpose Extraction – SPIES – training with a USAF MH-60 Pave Hawk.

Rangers and other special forces needing to be quickly pulled out of a confined area use SPIES – or Special Purpose Extraction.

USAF special operations MH-53 Pave Low seen ripple-firing infra-red flares.

An MC130 Combat Talon air refuelling a USAF special forces MH-53 Pave Low. Both aircraft can deploy Rangers either by parachute, air-land or air assault.

(LPH), and Landing Helicopter Assault (LHA) ships, which carry around 2200 marines plus aviation support from Bell/Boeing MV-22 Osprey tilt-rotor aircraft and updated AH-1Z Cobra attack and UH-1Y helicopters. The Marine Corps is ready to deploy at very short notice, either independently or alongside the 18th Airborne Corps and Special Operations Command.

US Special Operations Command

On 1 December 1989 the Department of the Army established the US Army Special Operations Command (USASOC) at Fort Bragg as a major initiative to enhance the readiness of Army special operations forces. The move helped to streamline command and control of all Army special operations including the Ranger Regiment, which in turn came under the US Special Operations Command (USSOCOM) located at Mac Dill Air Force Base in Florida. USSOCOM is the unified command for all US special operations, including Army, Air Force and Navy units.

US Army 75th Ranger Regiment

Activated as part of the US Army Special Operations Command in 1973, the 75th Ranger Regiment is its premier rapid-deployment, direct-action force. Undertaking a range of special missions, Rangers are trained for deployment by air, land or sea, and have been involved in many recent United States' operations including those to Grenada, Panama, Somalia, and also the Gulf War, and were the first units sent in.

All Rangers are volunteers. All officers and enlisted men must meet tough physical, mental and moral criteria. Officers and NCOs must be qualified in the art of airborne warfare, and be highly proficient in the roles they wish to perform.

All Rangers are trained in parachute air assault and Ranger skills at the regiment's school at Fort Benning, Georgia. The course involves the US Army's most comprehensive instruction in special operations and light infantry skills, covering desert, jungle and waterborne operations. The school graduates more than 1000 Rangers each year. Before attending the school, junior enlisted soldiers undertake pre-Ranger training to ensure they are mentally and physically prepared.

Once assigned to the Regiment, officers and senior NCOs attend the Ranger Orientation programme to integrate them into the regiment, while enlisted soldiers undertake a Ranger indoctrination programme to help assess individual physical qualifications.

Operating in the light infantry direct-action role for special operations, Rangers are also trained to sieze airfields, to undertake special raids in urban combat and in national evacuation operations, as well as how to recover personnel and special equipment.

Each Ranger battalion comprises 580 personnel

Fast-roping is one of the most common methods used by special operations personnel. Here para-jumpers are seen roping from a USAF MH-53 Pave Low.

assigned to three rifle companies and a headquarters company; each rifle company is made up of about 152 personnel. Ranger battalions are light infantry, and have only a few specialised vehicles and manned weapons systems. Standard weapons are small arms and light automatic weapons, along with 60 mm mortars and 84 mm Ranger anti-tank weapons.

Rangers work alongside other US Army special forces, and have their own helicopter support provided by the 160th Special Operations Aviation Regiment (Airborne), which operates a fleet of modified Boeing MH-47D/MH-47E Chinooks, Sikorsky MH-60K Black Hawks, and Boeing MH-6 Little Birds. These special operations aviators are trained for long-range clandestine missions, mainly operating at night. These include attack support, reconnaissance, troop transport and urban operations – in fact, anywhere they are needed.

Special forces and Rangers can also call upon the USAF Special Operations Command Sikorsky MH-53J Pave helicopter, MC-130E Combat Talon, and AC130 gunships to support them in combat.

75th Ranger Regiment – headquarters, Ranger School, Fort Benning, Georgia
1st Battalion, 75th Ranger Regiment – Hunter Army Airfield, Georgia
2nd Battalion, 75th Ranger Regiment – Fort Lewis, Washington
3rd Battalion, 75th Ranger Regiment – Fort Benning, Georgia

Each Ranger battalion numbers around 600 men, based around three rifle companies plus battalion headquarters. All are airborne-trained and are always ready for immediate deployment anywhere around the world using USAF transport aircraft such as the C-141 Starlifter, C-5 Galaxy, and C-17 Globemaster III for air- and or airborne assaults.

160th Special Operations Aviation Regiment (Airborne)

Based at Fort Campbell, Kentucky, the 160th SOAR(A) is the US Army's premier aviation regiment dedicated to supporting Special Operations Command.

After Operation *Eagle Claw*, the failed hostage rescue mission to Tehran in 1980, President Carter set up a commission to review US special operations activities; up until then the various services had been operating independently. The commission recommended that a special operations force should be established, under a single command with dedicated aircraft and crews capable of undertaking missions anywhere during peace or war, and

which would remain at a high state of readiness for immediate operations.

The US Army, Air Force and Navy established their own special forces groups under the overall command of a Joint Special Operations Command (JSOC) located at Fort Bragg. Using modified aircraft, each service developed its own special operations fixed-wing and helicopter units.

The 160th SOAR was created from elements of the 101st Airborne Division (Air Assault), which became the 160th Aviation Battalion in 1981, and the 160th Special Operations Aviation Group in 1986. Based at Fort Campbell, Kentucky, and Hunter Army Airfield, Savannah, the 160th SOAR operates modified special operations MH-60K Black Hawks, AH-6 Little Birds, and MH-46E Chinooks in support of a range of Army special forces. The 160th also operates modified MH-47D Chinooks and MH-60L Black Hawks along with the AH-60L Black Hawk direct action penetrator, a heavily-armed gunship.

The 160th has seen action in many recent US operations including Operation *Urgent Fury* in Grenada in October 1983; this was the first time its modified MH-60 Black Hawks and MH/AH-6 Little Birds were deployed.

The 160th spent hours practising night operations using night vision goggles and forward-looking infra-red systems, becoming the world's leading unit at this type of night-time aviation and earning the tag 'Night Stalkers'.

The 160th saw action again during Operation *Just Cause* in Panama in December 1989, when they quickly deployed from Savannah to Panama using air-to-air refuelling. The next major operations were during the Gulf War of 1991 when elements of the 160th were sent to Saudi Arabia to undertake a range of special force support missions, including combat search and rescue. The 160th were in action again in August 1993, when elements went to Somalia to support the 3rd Battalion, 75th Ranger Regiment and special operations Delta Force personnel. It also took part in Operation *Restore Democracy*, the US peace-keeping mission to Haiti in September 1994, and in the peace-keeping operation in Kosovo.

160th SOAR, Fort Campbell, Kentucky/Hunter Army airfield, Savannah, Georgia

1st Battalion, 160th SOAR: Fort Campbell, Kentucky: MH-60K/AH-60K Black Hawks and MH-6 Little Birds
2nd Battalion, 16th SOAR: Fort Campbell, Kentucky: MH-47E/MH-47D Chinooks
3rd Battalion, 160th SOAR: Hunter Army airfield; MH-60L/MH-60K Black Hawks based at Hunter Army airfield to work alongside 1st Battalion, 75th Ranger Regiment (Airborne)

CHAPTER 10
101st Airborne Division (Air Assault)

On 4 October 1974, the 101st Airborne Division (Air Assault) swapped parachutes for helicopters and became the first air assault division in the world. Based at Fort Campbell, Kentucky, the 101st became known as the Screaming Eagles from their Bald Eagle patch first adopted in 1923. It is the US Army's most powerful division, and is assigned to the 18th Airborne Corps rapid deployment force.

An air assault school was set up in 1974 to establish the standards necessary to develop the combined arms concept of air assault. Known as the Ten Toughest Days In The Army, the school at Fort Campbell has earned a worldwide reputation for excellence; thousands of soldiers, male and female as well as foreign military personnel, graduate from it. All members of the Air Assault Division, including aircrew, have to graduate from the school. The challenging curriculum includes all aspects of air assault operations, from combat to rigging techniques and rappelling.

The famous Bald Eagle emblem of the 101st worn on dress uniform.

Combat badge Screaming Eagle worn on battle dress uniforms (BDU) of the 101st Airborne Division.

OPPOSITE: An honour guard from 101st Airborne Division during a ceremony at their headquarters at Fort Campbell, Kentucky.

Air assault is not just the movement of troops from one location to another by helicopter, but a combined arms operation involving highly mobile troops on land or in the air. It is supported at all times by air reconnaissance and attack helicopters. The 'habitual association' policy ensures that the same units work regularly together, thereby increasing the overall effectiveness of the whole team. As an important and powerful asset on the modern battlefield, the Air Assault Division can operate anywhere in the world at short notice, undertaking a full range of missions. This was evident during the Gulf War when Apache helicopters of the 101st Airborne Division (Air Assault) carried out the famous raid into Iraq on the first night of the ground war.

As part of the US Army's rapid deployment force, the division can deploy by sea, land or air; a battalion-size unit can deploy within 12 hours, and a brigade-size force within 18 hours, including aviation and support units. The division with its fleet of 400 helicopters can be airlifted out of Campbell army airfield, one of the largest and busiest military airfields in the US. The division regularly practises loading its helicopters and equipment aboard USAF transport aircraft.

The division is flexible, and can move around a battlefield area regardless of terrain, reinforcing key positions or conducting deep-strike missions behind enemy lines. It is increasingly turning towards night operations, and almost all training missions are now conducted under cover of darkness.

The key elements of the division are its three infantry brigades. Each has a headquarters plus three battalions with more than 200 long-range Humvees or Hummers (high mobility multi-purpose wheeled vehicles).

Supporting the infantry brigades is the aviation brigade. This has three air assault helicopter battalions equipped with UH-60L Black Hawks, one medium-lift battalion of CH-47D Chinooks, two attack battalions armed with Boeing AH-64A/D Apaches, an air cavalry squadron of OH-58D/AH-64s, and a command and control/utility battalion, served by UH-60L Black Hawks.

A Black Hawk from A Co/6 Battalion, 101st Airborne Division flying in a 105 mm howitzer from 1st/320th Field Artillery Regiment.

A soldier from 101st Airborne Division covering the arrival of a 105 mm howitzer by a UH-60 Black Hawk.

The division's artillery comprises a headquarters battalion with three 105 mm howitzer battalions plus a 155 mm howitzer battalion used for general support.

Combat support command is made up of a maintenance, supply and transport battalion, an aviation maintenance unit, and a medical section, which includes an air ambulance company equipped with sixty UH-60 Black Hawk Medevac helicopters.

101st Airborne Division (Air Assault)
Infantry Brigades
1st Brigade: 1st, 2nd, 3rd, Battalions, 327th Infantry Regiment

2nd Brigade: 1st, 2nd, 3rd, Battalions, 502nd Infantry Regiment
3rd Brigade: 1st, 2nd, 3rd, Battalions, 187th Infantry Regiment
Divisional artillery
1st, 2nd, 3rd, Battalions, 320th Field Artillery Regiment (105 mm howitzers)
Battery C, 1st Battalion, 377th Field Artillery Regiment (155 mm howitzers)
2nd Field Artillery Detachment

101st Aviation Brigade/159th Aviation Brigade
The Aviation Brigade was formed on 1 July 1968 at Camp Eagle, Vietnam, as the 160th Aviation Group. In 1969 it was redesignated as the 101st Aviation Group with the emergence of airmobile battle doctrines. In August 1986, the 101st became the 101st Aviation Brigade, and in October 1987, it became regimentally affiliated.

The brigade leads the way in Army aviation innovations, and was the first to re-equip with the Black Hawk UH-60 and Chinook CH-47D helicopters, along with the updated AH-64D Apache.

The mobility that the Aviation Brigade gives to the division allows it to attack armoured forces and other hard targets, as well as the quick reinforcement of key positions and the execution of deep-strike missions. Every item of equipment in the division can be flown in or under its helicopters.

The brigade is ready to be deployed anywhere in the world within 36 hours as part of a joint, multi-national or unilateral task force.

101st Aviation Brigade – Sabre army airfield
101st Aviation Brigade
Headquarters company
2nd Squadron, 17th Cavalry Regiment (OH-58D Kiowa Warrior/AH-64 A/D Apache)
1st Battalion, 101st Aviation Regiment (AH-64A/D Apache)
2nd Battalion, 101st Aviation Regiment (AH-64A/D Apache)
3rd Battalion, 101st Aviation Regiment (AH-64A/D Apache)
6th Battalion, 101st Aviation Regiment (UH-60L Black Hawk)

159th Aviation Brigade – Campbell army airfield
4th Battalion, 101st Aviation Regiment (UH-60L Black Hawk)
5th Battalion, 101st Aviation Regiment (UH-60L Black Hawk)
7th Battalion, 101st Aviation Regiment (CH-47D Chinook)
9th Battalion, 101st Aviation Regiment (UH-60L Black Hawk)

The role of the 101st Aviation Brigade is to deploy worldwide; locate, identify and destroy enemy forces in joint, combined or unilateral operations; and deliver the men and equipment of the 101st Airborne Division to the battlefield.

A UH-60' Black Hawk seen carrying a high mobility, multi-purpose wheeled vehicle (HMMWV or Hummer). The Black Hawk is the workhorse of the Air Assault Division.

TOW missile-armed Hummer vehicle of 3/502nd Infantry. The Hummer can be used for a variety of missions and like the Black Hawk is the ground workhorse of the 101st Airborne Division.

Members of the 101st Airborne Division reconnaissance unit seen undertaking stabilised tactical airborne body operations (STABO).

A Medevac Black Hawk from D Company, 326th Medical Battalion undertakes the 'Dust-Off' missions for the 101st Airborne Division including Combat SAR missions for downed aircrew. They are all night vision goggle trained.

ABOVE: *A 'killer Junior' fired by a 105 mm howitzer of 320th Artillery Battalion. They are fired on a horizontal trajectory with a fuse timed to explode the shell at around 150 yards. They are excellent for perimeter security.*

BELOW: *Just a small part of the flight line for 101st Airborne Division at Campbell army airfield. The Division has over 300 combat helicopters.*

ABOVE: *War art seen at the entrance to 1-101st. This unit operates the AH-64A/D Apache.*

RIGHT: *An Apache pilot from 1-101st prepares for a night mission from Sabre army airfield. The integrated helmet and display system (IHADSS) monocle can be clearly seen. This displays a thermal image of the outside world plus flight/weapons/target data information onto the pilot's right eye.*

ABOVE: *The flight line at Sabre army airfield located on the Training Reservation at Fort Campbell and home to 1-101st and 2nd Squadron, 17th Cavalry Regiment, 101st Airborne Division. The squadrons operate a mixture of OH-58s; AH-64 A/Ds and AH-1s.*

LEFT: *A flight of Apache AH-64As from 1-101st Airborne heading out for a night deep-strike mission from Fort Campbell.*

ABOVE: *An aviation battalion commander briefs an OH-58 pilot prior to a mission at Fort Campbell.*

BELOW: *Almost every item of combat equipment with the 101st Airborne Division is capable of being flown by their helicopters. The air assault soldiers continually train with their aviation units day and night.*

All the aviation units within the 101st Airborne Division regularly field deploy alongside the air assault troops and undertake the habitual association philosophy in training.

CHAPTER 11
82nd Airborne Division

K nown as America's Guard of Honour, the 82nd Airborne Division is the largest parachute force in the world. Every member is airborne qualified. Furthermore, almost every piece of equipment they use can be dropped by parachute onto the battlefield.

The 82nd Airborne Division is trained to deploy anywhere in the world within 18 hours of being notified. With its own helicopter support, the division can conduct a full range of missions. These include parachute assaults, forcible entry operations, capture of enemy and airfields. There are also spearhead operations, where the division can build up its combat power quickly, and conduct follow-on missions either independently or as part of a combined or multi-national force.

As an important element of the US Strategic Rapid Reaction Corps the 82nd Airborne Division is one of four assigned to the 18th Airborne Corps, which also includes the 3rd Infantry Division (Mechanised), 10th Mountain Division (Light), and the 101st Airborne Division (Air Assault). These Divisions, plus Special Operations Command, form the rapid reaction force, and have all seen action in theatres including Grenada, Panama, Haiti, the Gulf War, Bosnia and Somalia.

82nd Airborne Division

Comprising around 18 000 personnel, the 82nd Airborne Division was formed in 1917, and became known as the

A Chinook from C Company 159th Battalion over-flies Simmons army airfield at Fort Bragg, home to the 82nd Airborne Division.

ABOVE: *An AH-64A from 1/159th Attack Aviation Regiment seen at Simmons AAF, Fort Bragg.*

BELOW: *A CH-47D Chinook from C Company 159th Battalion deploying troops from 82nd Airborne Division at Fort Bragg.*

'All Americans' because the personnel were recruited from all over the country. Its red, white and blue shoulder flash, bearing the letters AA, has been worn ever since.

The division is based around three airborne infantry brigades with their own artillery, aviation, combat support, and specialist units, which can be deployed as a whole or in part depending on the mission. The division relies on the USAF mobility airlift command's C-5 Galaxies, C-141 Starlifters, C-17 Globemasters and C130 Hercules to help it reach combat areas abroad, and uses its own helicopters once on the ground.

Troops are trained at the US Army's Parachute Training School at Fort Benning, and once qualified maintain their combat and airborne readiness by attending the 82nd Airborne Division's Advanced Airborne School at Fort Bragg.

The school trains selected personnel in jumpmaster, air movement and basic airborne techniques, and advises and assists unit commanders in the evaluation of jumpmasters and air movement officers and NCOs.

82nd Airborne Division Units

1st Brigade, 504th Parachute Infantry Regiment
2nd Brigade, 325th Airborne Infantry Regiment
3rd Brigade, 505th Parachute Infantry Regiment
82nd Aviation Brigade, 1–82nd Aviation Regiment (Attack),
    1–17th Cavalry Squadron (OH-58D), 2–82nd Aviation
    Regiment (UH-60L Black Hawk), plus C Company, 159th
    Aviation Regiment (Chinook)
307th Engineer Battalion
82nd Soldier Support Battalion
313th Military Intelligence Battalion
82nd Military Police Company
Division Support Command
Advanced Airborne School
Division G1/AG

The division can also call upon units of the 18th Airborne Corps, which include: 3rd Infantry Division (Mechanised); 10th Mountain Division (Light); 101st Airborne Division (Air Assault); 1st Corps Support Command; 18th Airborne Corps Artillery; 44th Medical Brigade; 2nd Armoured Cavalry Regiment; 16th Military Police Brigade (Airborne); 18th Soldier Support Group; 20th Engineer Brigade (Combat Airborne); 35th Signal Brigade (Airborne); 108th Air Defence Artillery Brigade; 525th Military Intelligence Brigade (Airborne); and Dragon Brigade. 18th Airborne Corps' assets also include the 229th Aviation Regiment, and the 18th Aviation Brigade headquarters company, 1st/58th Aviation Regiment, C Company 159th Aviation Regiment and 1st/159th Attack Aviation Regiment.

Airborne troops board a Chinook from 18th Aviation Brigade during an exercise in the UK. The 82nd Airborne Division regularly deploys abroad for exercises.

LEFT: *The front office of an 18th Aviation Brigade CH-47D Chinook.*

BELOW: *Black Hawks and Chinooks lined-up at Fort Bragg ready to fly out the soldiers of 82nd Airborne Division after a massed parachute jump.*

RIGHT: *The Chinook is the workhorse of the US Army, especially the airborne and air assault units.*

BELOW: *The crew of the Command and Control Black Hawk used by the airborne commander of 82nd Airborne Division ready to depart for a mission. The extra fuel tanks allow the Black Hawk several more hours of flight time.*

ABOVE: *A Chinook flies soldiers of 82nd Airborne Division from the drop-zone to their patrol area during an exercise.*

BELOW: *An 82nd Aviation Division Medevac Black Hawk seen departing Simmons AAF.*

ABOVE: *USAF C-141 Starlifters are used by the 82nd Airborne Division to deploy worldwide either by air-land or parachute assaults.*

RIGHT: *A Chinook pilot from 18th Aviation Brigade shows his ANVIS 7 NVGs. All the pilots in the Brigade are NVG qualified in support of the 82nd Airborne Division.*

LEFT: *The 82nd Airborne Division has its own field artillery units who operate 105 mm howitzers that can be parachuted into theatre or flown in by their helicopters.*

BELOW: *The nose of a Medevac UH-60 Black Hawk from 57th Medical Battalion based at Fort Bragg.*

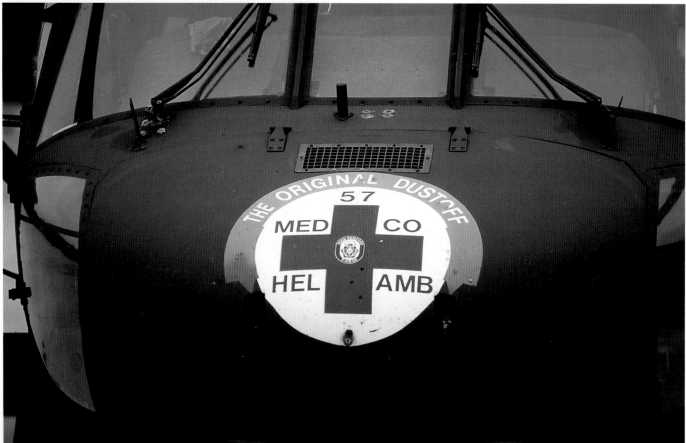

ABOVE: *A C-141 Starlifter along with the C-5 Galaxy and C-17 Globemaster allows the 82nd Airborne Division to deploy worldwide within 18 hours.*

BELOW: *The new C-17 Globemaster III will replace the USAF fleet of ageing C-141 Starlifters and C-5 Galaxy airlifters and also provide the UK with their future rapid deployment airlift requirements.*

CHAPTER 12
European Rapid Reaction Force (ERRF)

In 1991 it was decided that under the framework of Nato, an airmobile division would be formed from four of the European 'central region' nations. This new division would be assigned to Nato's Allied Command Europe (ACE) Rapid Reaction Corps and form a large part of the ACE mobile force.

The ACE force, or Allied Mobile Force (AMF), is composed of land and air forces drawn from Nato nations – Belgium, Canada, France, Germany, Italy, Luxembourg, the Netherlands, the UK and the United States. The original ACE force, when fully deployed, comprised infantry battalions, artillery batteries and supporting units, with a fighting strength of a brigade group of about 5000 men.

Its success prompted the creation of the airmobile division in January 1992, when the ministers of defence of the participating countries (the UK, Belgium, Germany and the Netherlands) signed a memorandum of understanding to establish the MND (C) Airmobile Division. Each of the four nations provided one airmobile brigade. These were:

UK: 24 Airmobile Brigade – now 16 Air Assault Brigade
Belgium: Para Commando Brigade based at Heverlee
Germany: 31 *Luftland* Brigade based at Oldenburg
Netherlands: 11 Airmobile Brigade based at Arnhem

Dutch 11 Airmobile Brigade troops board a German Army CH-53D from 35 Regiment during a joint Nato exercise.

ABOVE: Hellfire missiles and rocket dispenser fitted to a brand-new Dutch Air Force Boeing AH-64D Apache.

BELOW: A German Army 35 Regiment CH-53D working alongside a Dutch Air Force Eurocopter Cougar from 300 Squadron during exercise Artful Issue; the first major European airmobile exercise.

European Rapid Reaction Force (ERRF)

The idea for the ERRF was conceived at a meeting in Brussels on 20 November 2000, and confirmed at a European ministers' meeting in Nice early the following month. With 2003 set as the operational target date, the member states pledged around 100 000 troops, 400 combat aircraft and 100 ships. This new 15-nation European multi-national rapid reaction force, made up of many of the nations already assigned to Nato, will be capable of operating under European directives without the involvement of the US. The new force will contribute to the EU's common foreign and security policy, and undertake a variety of missions. These include supplying humanitarian aid, evacuation in the aftermath of a natural catastrophe, peace-keeping duties, direct intervention to separate warring sides and to restore peace, and protecting European interests.

During deployments involving a force some 60 000 strong, the new rapid reaction force will be capable of deploying for a variety of operations within sixty days, and sustain them for between six months and a year. It will include air, land, amphibious and other maritime units.

UK: 24 000 personnel including 12 500 troops, 72 aircraft and 18 warships. Both the 16 Air Assault Brigade and Amphibious Task Group will be involved along with RAF Eurofighter and C-17 Globemaster III transport aircraft.

France: 12 000 troops plus aircraft, ships and helicopters. Will include amphibious and airmobile units, such as the *4ème Division Aéromobile*.

Germany: 12 000 troops plus aircraft, ships and helicopters, along with 31 *Luftland* Brigade.

Italy: 12 000 troops plus aircraft, ships and helicopters, including the San Marco Battalion.

Spain: 6000 troops plus aircraft, ships and helicopters. Will

Dutch Air Force C130 Hercules arriving at Delaan airfield to load UK and Dutch airmobile troops for a joint helicopter and air-land mission.

include the *Fuerza de Accion Rapida*, comprising *La Legion Española* and *Brigada Paracaidasta*.

Netherlands: 5000 soldiers plus aircraft, ships and helicopters. The 11th *Luchtmobiele Brigade* and Royal Netherlands Marine Corps will be involved.

Greece: 3000 soldiers plus aircraft, ships and helicopters.

Austria: 2000 soldiers plus aircraft and S-70 Black Hawk helicopters.

Sweden: 1500 soldiers.

Norway: 1500.

Finland: 1500.

Portugal: 1059.

Belgium: 1000 soldiers, including Para Commando Brigade, plus aircraft.

Denmark: 1000.

Ireland: 850.

Luxembourg: 100.

Other European non-EU members have also expressed an interest in participating in the new force. They include: Poland, Hungary, the Czech Republic, Turkey, Bulgaria, Cyprus, Estonia, Latvia, Lithuania, Malta, Romania, Slovakia and Slovenia.

ABOVE: *A 35 Regiment, German Army CH-53D flying forward a Dutch 11 Airmobile Brigade command vehicle during exercise* Artful Issue *held in Holland in October 2000.*

BELOW: *Dutch Air Force personnel from No 302 Squadron prepare one of their new Boeing Apache AH-64Ds at a field side for an escort mission during exercise* Artful Issue.

ABOVE: *A Dutch Air Force 298 Squadron CH-47D Chinook lifting an 11 Airmobile Brigade command vehicle and satellite communications system forward during an airmobile assault by UK, German, Dutch and Belgian troops.*

BELOW: *During the early 1990s the Dutch began to modernise their helicopter fleet for future airmobile operations including buying new Chinook CH-47Ds, Apache AH-64Ds and updating their Navy Lynx. A 298 Squadron Chinook is seen lifting 20 mm mortars for 11 Airmobile Brigade.*

ABOVE: *As well as buying a fleet of Chinooks the Dutch also bought 17 new Eurocopter Cougars operated by 300 Squadron based at Soesterberg.*

BELOW: *A Dutch Air Force 302 Squadron technician checks the avionics bay of a new Boeing Apache AH-64D. The Dutch have bought 30 new Apache AH-64Ds.*

ABOVE: *The glass cockpit of a 300 Squadron Cougar, showing colour multifunction displays.*

LEFT: *Eight of the new Dutch Eurocopter Cougars are fitted with flotation equipment for operations aboard their new Landing Platform Dock (LPD) HNLMS Rotterdam.*

RIGHT: *11 Airmobile Brigade soldiers hook up a 20 mm mortar to a 298 Squadron Chinook CH-47D.*

BELOW: *British 16 Air Assault Brigade troops jogging over to their helicopter during exercise* Artful Issue. *Dutch and British Chinooks worked alongside German Army and Belgian helicopters.*

ABOVE: *A Dutch Air Force Boeing AH-64D Apache escorting Dutch and RAF Chinooks during an airmobile assault in Belgium.*

LEFT: *Prior to the arrival of their new AH-64D Apaches the Dutch leased ex-US Army AH-64A models. These returned to the USA at the end of 2000.*

ABOVE: *Dutch Chinook and two German CH-53Ds arriving at Delaan airfield in Holland to pick-up Dutch and British troops for an airmobile assault.*

BELOW: *Short finals to their home base at Soesterberg for a 298 Squadron Chinook CH-47D. The shot clearly shows the Dutch Chinook's new glass cockpit and colour multifunction displays.*

ABOVE: *German* Luftland *paratroopers jumping from a German Air Force C-160 Transal aircraft.*

BELOW: *German* Luftland *troops seen departing a CH-53D during a Nato exercise.*

Above: *Dutch 11 Airmobile Brigade troops carrying a casualty to an RAF Chinook during a Nato airmobile exercise.*

Below: *Belgian Para Commandos boarding a new RAF 18 Squadron Chinook HC2A at an airfield in Belgium during exercise Artful Issue. This airmobile exercise included the combined use of C130s and helicopters for major assaults.*

ABOVE: *The elements of a multi-national Euro force, seen together at Delaan airfield prior to a major air assault, included Dutch, British (Gurkha from 16 Air Assault Brigade) and Belgian troops preparing for a joint air assault mission.*

BELOW: *Dutch 11 Airmobile Brigade troops board an RAF 18 Squadron Chinook. Also a German 35 Regiment CH-53D lifts out a Dutch vehicle during a combined air assault mission.*

A Dutch Air Force Boeing CH-47D Chinook from 298 Squadron lifting out of a landing site.

ABOVE: *A Dutch Air Force 298 Squadron Chinook pilot checking a landing site prior to deploying British 16 Air Assault Brigade troops.*

BELOW: *French Commandos de L'Air wait to be moved by RAF helicopters.*

ABOVE: *British and French troops boarding RAF 7 Squadron Chinooks during a joint exercise.*

BELOW: *French Commandos de L'Air boarding an FAF C-160 Transal during a joint exercise in Wales.*

LEFT: *Dutch 11 Airmobile Brigade troops hooking-up 20 mm mortars with a 300 Squadron Cougar in the background.*

BELOW: *Spanish special forces board a Royal Navy 845 Naval Air Squadron Commando Sea King near Seville for a Combat SAR mission.*

A French Army ALAT Cougar Mk II seen lifting a Dutch 11 Airmobile Brigade vehicle.

Paratroopers form the spearhead of Spanish Army Rapid Reaction Force capabilities, which also include their La Legion Española.

The Spanish army aviation unit known as the FAMET operates a fleet of modernised CH-47D Chinooks.

BELOW: *A Spanish Army (FAMET) BHELTRA-V Boeing CH-47D Chinook lifting a 105 mm howitzer from a Spanish Army parachute battalion, part of their Rapid Reaction Force.*

Belgian Army Agusta A109 armed with TOW missile system departing to escort British, Dutch and German helicopters during exercise Artful Issue.

Belgian Army TOW-missile-armed Agusta A109s form the nucleus of Belgian Army aviation operating in the attack and reconnaissance role.

BELOW: The Belgian Army Agusta A109 can be used for TOW missiles or, by using the roof-mounted sighting system, for reconnaissance missions.

ABOVE: *The new Eurocopter Tiger is now entering service with both French and German Army units in large numbers.*

BELOW: *Spanish Army CH-47D lifting a pair a 105 mm howitzers in the mountains north of Madrid.*

ABOVE: *French Commando de L'Air paratroopers are all parachute trained and can deploy day or night.*

BELOW: *The French ALAT Gazelle will be replaced in the near future by the new Eurocopter Tiger.*

ABOVE: *French 4DAM Cougars and 20 mm cannon-armed Gazelles seen forward deployed during an airmobile exercise in France. 4DAMs are the major element of French Rapid Reaction Force and train for both land and amphibious missions.*

BELOW: *The new multi-role Eurocopter Tiger will be deployed in two variants, the UHT version (anti-tank missile roof-mounted sight) by the German Army and by the French ALAT in both the HAC version similar to the German UHT and HAP escort variant when armed with a nose-mounted cannon and roof sight.*

French ALAT 4DAM Puma seen in desert camouflage having returned from duties in Chad.

French 4DAM Gazelles fitted with HOT missile systems will be replaced by the new multi-role Tiger equipped with TRIGAT missile and HOT 2 system.

BELOW: *The latest Eurocopter Cougar Mk II operated by 4DAM, the workhorse of French airmobile and rapid deployment capabilities.*

LEFT: *4DAM Gazelles seen field-deployed with crews training for chemical/biological warfare, still a real threat in modern warfare.*

BELOW: *German Luftland Brigade Weasel armoured vehicle designed for airmobile operations and carried inside their C-160 Transals and CH-53Ds, seen here about to be loaded into an RAF Chinook.*

CHAPTER 13
US Marine Expeditionary Units

The US Marine Corps, known as The President's Own, can be deployed on the orders of the President without the sanction of Congress, and has, in the past, been the first into action working alongside its US Army counterparts, the 75th Ranger Regiment and 18th Airborne Corps.

A Marine expeditionary unit (MEU) is a small, powerful force with a strength of about 2200 personnel deployed on up to four ships. There is a marine battalion, and an air squadron including helicopters and Harriers, and support units, under a single commander.

Led by a colonel, units are constantly deployed around the world, with fleets in the Mediterranean, the western Pacific, and periodically the Atlantic and Indian Ocean.

US Marines hit the beach. The USMC regularly deploys worldwide as part of its rapid reaction concept of operations.

ABOVE: *The USS* Whidbey Island *(LSD-41) is designed to support amphibious assault operations and can launch loaded amphibious craft and vehicles and form part of a USMC marine expeditionary unit.*

BELOW: *A pair of CH-53Es from HMH-464 preparing to land during an assault mission.*

The ground combat element is the battalion landing team, an infantry battalion reinforced with artillery, amphibious assault vehicles, and light armoured reconnaissance units.

One of the most important assets of the Marine expeditionary unit is its aviation combat element based around the new Bell/Boeing MV-22 Osprey tilt-rotor aircraft, which provide the Marines with a huge improvement in their air assault capability. This type of aircraft is backed up by three other helicopter types, including the CH-53E Super Stallion, the AH-1Z Super Cobra, and the UH-1Y Huey. There may also be a squadron of AV-8B Harriers, which are to be replaced by the new short take-off and vertical landing (STOVL) variant of the joint strike fighter.

US Marine Corps Expeditionery Units

West Coast: Based at Camp Pendleton, California – 11th, 13th, and 15th MEUs

East Coast: Based at Camp Lejeune, North California – 22nd, 24th, and 26th MEUs

Overseas: Based at Okinawa, Japan – 31st MEU

There are at least three MEUs always at sea on six-month deployments.

US Marine Corps Aviation

The Marine Corps has begun to introduce three new aircraft, which will revolutionise its amphibious warfare doctrine. The Bell/Boeing MV-22B Osprey tilt-rotor aircraft successfully completed a series of trials in early 2000, and the first of an eventual 360 MV-22s became operational at the Marines' New River Station with VMMT-204, the MV-22 Osprey Training Squadron.

Bell AH-1Z and UH-1Y

On 20 November 2000, the first of 180 Bell AH-1Z attack helicopters rolled out of the Bell flight research centre in Arlington, Texas. The AH-1Z is an upgraded variant of the Bell AH-1W Cobra, part of an improvement programme referred to as H-1 that will also see the re-manufacture and update of 100 Bell UH-1N utility helicopters to the new UH-1Y configuration.

The H-1 programme will allow 280 new US Marine

The USS Bataan *is the latest Wasp Class amphibious assault ship capable of deploying a full Marine amphibious assault group plus their aviation units which will include the MV-22 Osprey.*

As part of their rapid reaction capability USMC CH-53Es regularly air refuel from Marine C130 Hercules to help extend their operational role and rapid deployment capabilities.

Corps aircraft to operate beyond 2020. Their airframes will have zero-time, and the latest technology. The speed, range, manoeuvrability and lift capability of these aircraft will be dramatically improved.

Improvements include the Litton Integrated Avionics system with 'glass-cockpit', multi-function displays; mission and weapons computers; and advanced communication and navigation systems. New GE-T700 engines, four-blade all composite, hingeless, bearingless main-rotors, identical drive trains, hydraulics and electrical systems. The first AH-1Z took flight in December 2000, followed by the UH-1Y in early 2001. Deliveries to the Marine Corps begin in 2004.

Bell/Boeing MV-22 Osprey

The MV-22 Osprey, capable of taking off and landing like a helicopter and also flying like a turbo-prop, provides twice the speed, five times the range and can lift three times the payload of the Boeing CH-46E Sea Knight it is replacing. With the Bell AH-1Z and UH-1Y, the Marine Corps is well placed to expand its amphibious warfare policy at greater distances than ever.

These new aircraft will form the nucleus of the Marines' global rapid reaction capabilities. It is intended that the MV-22 will eventually work alongside the CH-53E Super Stallion and AH-1Z/UH-1Y.

The Osprey is crewed by a pilot and co-pilot, and can carry twenty-four fully-equipped Marines, or twelve stretchers. Twin external hooks allow a load of almost 10 000 lb to be carried at speeds of up to 200 knots. In the conventional aircraft role, the MV-22 can cruise at 316 knots, has a service ceiling of more than 25 000 ft, and a range of more than 515 nautical miles.

Designed for on-ship operations, the Osprey's wings and blades can be stowed to allow access onto aircraft lifts. During operational service, there will be twelve MV-22s embarked as part of an aviation combat element, working alongside the CH-53E, AH-1Z and UH-1Y. Air-to-air refuelling from C130 Hercules allows the Osprey greater flexibility.

A US Navy Landing Craft Air Cushion (LCAC) from the USS Bataan *deploys an M1 Abrams main battle tank to the beachhead.*

ABOVE: *Brought to the beach by the LCAC, a USMC amphibious armoured vehicle prepares to disembark its load of Marines.*

BELOW: *The LCAC can travel over land and sea at over 40 knots carrying a 75-ton load.*

The US Navy LCAC can carry a variety of loads including troops and vehicles and along with helicopters provides the US Marine Corps with its long-range amphibious assault capability.

OPPOSITE: *The busy flight deck of the USS* Bataan, *which can operate both helicopters and Harrier AV-8Bs.*

BELOW: *The USS* Bataan *can carry over 2000 Marines plus a full Aviation Combat Element including Harrier AV-8s and soon the MV-22 Osprey along with four LCACs which operate from the aft well-deck.*

ABOVE: *After the fatal accident in the autumn of 2000 at MCAS New River, the MV-22 Osprey will continue to be produced and should enter service with the USMC in the next few years.*

BELOW: *The USMC continue to support the MV-22 Osprey which will provide them with their air assault capabilities throughout the next thirty years along with USAF Special Operations.*

CHAPTER 14
UK Amphibious Task Group

As part of the UK's rapid reaction capability, the Amphibious Task Group holds the position of spearhead rapid reaction unit, along with 16 Air Assault Brigade.

The ATG comprises 3 Commando Brigade and the Royal Navy Amphibious Force based on HMS *Ocean* and two new Landing Platform Docks (LPD), HMS *Albion* and HMS *Bulwark*.

HMS *Ocean,* which entered service in August 1999, is the spearhead of the Royal Navy's amphibious force. It is capable of carrying a Commando group of 803, along with their equipment, plus a Tailored Air Group of twelve support helicopters. These include the Sea King, Lynx AH7, Merlin and Apache.

Royal Marines board an RAF Chinook and Commando Sea King for an air assault from HMS Ocean.

ABOVE: *847 Naval Air Squadron Lynx and 845/846 Naval Air Squadron Commando Sea Kings lined-up on the deck of HMS Ocean.*

BELOW: *Royal Marines board an 18 Squadron RAF Chinook in the Egyptian desert to be flown back to HMS Ocean. Marines regularly train in desert, jungle and arctic environments.*

ABOVE: *The RAF Chinook is now part of the UK's Amphibious Tailored Air Group operating from HMS* Ocean *in support of amphibious operations.*

BELOW: *HMS* Ocean *has given the UK a global amphibious rapid reaction capability, deploying helicopter support and 1000 marines plus landing craft.*

ABOVE: *Commando Sea Kings and Lynx operating from HMS* Ocean's *six-spot deck.*

BELOW: *Two new Landing Platform Docks HMS* Bulwark *and* Albion *form the core of the UK's Amphibious Task Group and will soon join HMS* Ocean.

HMS Ocean *can operate a mix of Commando Sea Kings and Lynx helicopters plus the new Merlin helicopter.*

ABOVE: *As well as operating a mix of Commando Sea Kings and Lynx helicopters HMS* Ocean *now deploys with two RAF Chinooks. The new Apache AH1 will also be embarked.*

BELOW: *This image clearly shows the six-spot deck with four Sea Kings and a Chinook plus a large deck lift.*

OPPOSITE: *Egyptian paratroopers being transported to the flight deck to board their RAF Chinook and to be flown ashore during multi-national exercise Bright Star 99 in Egypt.*

ABOVE: *An RAF Chinook departs the deck of HMS Ocean. The Chinook is now part of the ship's Tailored Air Group and will soon be joined by the Army Apache AH1.*

BELOW: *A pair of 846 Naval Air Squadron Commando Sea Kings having flown from HMS Ocean prepares to deploy Marines ashore in Egypt.*

CHAPTER 15
Global Rapid Reaction Aircraft

Today's military policy increasingly involves the use of technology to help it meet its aims. The United States has begun to develop long-range unmanned vehicles for intelligence gathering and surveillance. The next step will see hunter-killer teams with armed unmanned aerial vehicles (UAVs) controlled by manned aircraft or helicopters.

The ability to fire precision-guided bombs from a distance was highlighted during the 1999/2000 bombing of Serbia, with B2 bombers from the US working alongside Stealth bombers. The ability to deliver precision strikes prior to the arrival of ground troops will be vital in future conflicts.

The Globemaster III, which entered service with the RAF in May 2001, is now the main airlifter for the UK's rapid reaction force.

The Northrop Grumman B-2 can undertake precision bombing using laser-guided bombs anywhere on the globe operating from US bases. This will provide a valuable capability for US forces undertaking expeditionary type missions far from home.

ABOVE: *The F-117A Nighthawk when refuelled in the air from a KC-135R Stratotanker can penetrate enemy air defences and undertake precision bombing guided in by special forces.*

LEFT: *During 2000 the Global Hawk shattered the world endurance record for jet-powered unmanned vehicles when it flew a 31.5-hour mission. The Global Hawk can undertake reconnaissance missions anywhere in the world providing real-time imagery.*

BELOW: *Unmanned aerial vehicles like the Dark Star will soon be armed and will be controlled by manned aircraft to undertake more dangerous bombing and surveillance missions.*

LEFT: *The US military Air Mobility Command is the backbone of the US rapid reaction capability using a fleet of C-5 Galaxy and C-17 Globemaster III aircraft.*

BELOW: *The Boeing C-17 Globemaster III transport aircraft is the premier airlifter for the US rapid global mobility, undertaking both strategic and tactical airlift capabilities.*

INDEX

Note: Illustrations are indicated by *italic* page numbers. There may also be textual references on these pages.